# Another Me

# Another Me

A Memoir by

## Ann Montgomery

**Another Me**

Copyright © 2008 by Ann Montgomery

iUniverse books may be ordered through booksellers or by contacting:

iUniverse
1663 Liberty Drive
Bloomington, IN 47403
www.iuniverse.com
1-800-Authors (1-800-288-4677)

ISBN: 978-0-595-52298-9 (pbk)
ISBN: 978-0-595-62353-2 (ebk)

Printed in the United States of America


iUniverse rev. date: 11/25/08

*For Brock and our five children.*

# Table of Contents

# 1
## First Takes

September 1954

Acrowd of passengers milled around the Hoboken dock, waiting for the gangplank to be let down. The Ryndam, a stocky Holland America steamship, its gray hull pockmarked with black portholes, rode stolidly at bay. Red and black stripes on the smokestack painted a brave smear of color against the pewter sky. A knife-edged, cold September rain began to fall, but unpromising weather could not alter the excitement I felt as I contemplated my first ocean voyage. The dream of freedom and the allure of foreign travel were all the traveling companions I needed. For the first time in my twenty-two years, I was on my own, both observer and actor in my own script. With the ink still wet on my bachelor's diploma, I was going to France, venturing into cultural limbo, leaving the confines and comforts of my small Ohio college town. Paris would be the reward for my invention of a new self.

There is a tall young woman, thin as a shadow, standing alone beside her shiny black footlocker addressed to *Pension des Grandes Écoles, 75 rue du Cardinal Lemoine*, Paris,

1

France. She is holding the wide opera collar of her long black coat closed with two hands. The hem covers the tops of her woolen kneesocks, showing her plain brown leather penny loafers. Her light brown hair is neatly bobbed, her oval face with its wide-set blue eyes and aquiline nose perfectly framed by a straight fringe of bangs. She fidgets a bit, clutching the wide collar tighter around her neck, stamping her feet, waiting for a place in line.

I know every landmark, street and tree of Oxford, the Ohio college town where her journey began. The secrets and tedium of her youth are my familiars. When the boat sails for France, I will go with it because this girl—*C'est moi.*

\* \* \* \*

In 1954, a one-way fare from New York to Le Havre by steamship was a modest one hundred eight-five dollars. The ticket was the first installment of my Uncle Kenneth's generous travel loan to me. Kenneth, one of my father's four brothers, a partner in the then-honest Arthur Andersen accounting firm, could afford to help me as my father, a classics professor, claimed he could not. The Fulbright scholarship I had applied for just before graduation from college went to a more academically accomplished French major. But I was determined to go to Paris and live. Nothing could stop me, certainly not the simple fact that I had no money. Despite part-time jobs during high school and college, with full-time summer jobs as well, I had graduated penniless. My uncle agreed to give me the steamship ticket and an additional three hundred dollars in traveler's checks to sustain me until I found a job. A well-traveled professor in my French Department had assured me I could live for three months on that sum. Though the ten-day ocean voyage often seemed an eternity, it gave me time and leisure to meet other passengers, mostly students headed for a year of foreign study, plus a few future expatriates. The shipboard friendships, as much as the three hundred dollars in traveler's checks, would became the foundation of my life in Paris. That small floating world was my first safe harbor.

At the top of the gangplank, a Dutch sailor in navy turtleneck and trousers picked up my luggage as if it were feather light. The footlocker and a small suitcase would magically appear later in my cabin. But there were no bouquets of flowers or bon voyage telegrams to mark the beginning of the voyage. My father had often tried to discourage my flights to an independent adult life. I had lived at home even while I attended college, at his insistence—he claimed that campus room and board would be too expensive. He was blinded to my bitter disappointment as I watched my friends leave home for college and became isolated from my more fortunate peers. Or maybe that was the point. It is not surprising that he ignored my sailing date.

As I stood on deck, gazing mournfully at the darkening sky and darker water, Holland America's roving photographer asked if I would pose for a picture. Numbed by my own anxieties and reveries, I nodded yes and was paraded to a spot in front of a life preserver. The photographer, a short young man with surprising enthusiasm for his mundane job, was the only person noticing my departure. For more of a traveler's flair, he suggested that I open the front of my wrap coat, as if a brisk wind had already set me afloat. He placed my purse in my left hand, bending my arm to hold it in place as if I were an inanimate puppet. I had selected my black wool wrap coat from the sales rack at Jenny's, a chic emporium in Cincinnati that specialized in stylish women's clothes. Like everything else I did without his guidance, the eccentric purchase never got my father's approval. He suggested I would have been better dressed in tailored camelhair from Peck & Peck.

"Good! Hold that pose." I managed a brave smile for the camera, glad to have even a temporary distraction from my traveler's angst. After he clicked the shutter of his tripod camera several times, the photographer took my home address and promised to send the picture to the local newspaper.

"Are you traveling with friends?" he asked. By this time, my courage was beginning to falter and I resented being questioned. "What do you plan to do in Paris?" he continued, undeterred by my silence. I stubbornly refused to discuss my uncertain future plans. To break the silence I impulsively announced, "I'm going to study." Writing quickly in his small notebook, he finished my sentence for me. "Oh, yes, at the Sorbonne." I earnestly nodded my head. I had just acquired an important addendum to my passport. "*Je suis étudiante*" became my mantra. Months later, "I am a student" would follow the presentation of my passport each time I crossed the English Channel just before I ran for the train to London. The customs official would stamp "Passage permitted" on my passport, no more questions asked.

Two days after we sailed my photograph from the deck of the Ryndam appeared on the Society page of the *Hamilton* (Ohio) *Journal*, the only daily paper near Oxford. The bold caption: "Miss Ann Montgomery... on the deck of the Holland-American Liner, 'S.S. Ryndam' just before sailing from New York harbor, en route to Paris, France, where she will study

French literature at the Sorbonne." There were no fact checkers to question my invented claim of scholarly pursuits.

As the sound of foghorns penetrated the morning mist, the tugboats nosed the Ryndam down the Hudson River to the open Atlantic. The stacks sounded three parting blasts as the ship headed out the Narrows to Southampton and Le Havre. There were only a dozen second-class cabins on the small superior deck, and no first-class accommodations. Everyone else was double-bunked below deck, off narrow, dimly lit hallways that were particularly difficult to navigate after an evening in the ship's bar. I shared a tiny cabin on the lower deck with an elderly German woman who spoke no English. Since she was seasick for the entire trip and rarely left her bunk, we hardly spoke.

My suitcase was packed with my minimal winter wardrobe: two turtlenecks and one cardigan sweater, a straight skirt and a pair of slacks, underwear and a nightgown and robe. The footlocker with an extra pair of shoes, two jackets, a secondhand Olivetti portable typewriter, my small collection of French novels and a French grammar was shoved under my bunk.

Only a week before, at six in the morning, I had left my home on Oxford's Church Street and walked the short block to the bus station on the town square. The early September sun spilled over the square's park, its giant metal water tower, an Oxford landmark, casting a deep shadow over the grass. I was alone because my parents were unable or unwilling to watch the bus pull away from the curb on Park Place for the fourteen-hour trip to New York.

Five of my closest friends with whom I had grown up were married soon after college graduation. I was a bridesmaid in two of those weddings. By the time I finally left Oxford, they had all moved away, scattered across the country with their new husbands, babies soon to follow. They seemed to be happily living the American Dream while I was giving up it for the anonymity of a foreign land. My first attempt at independent life—six months spent working as a receptionist in New York instead of attending the second semester of my sophomore year—ended abruptly when my mother was hospitalized with what was termed a nervous breakdown. Her illness turned out to be far more serious than that, but the crisis was well-timed for me. I was called home to help my family and forced to finish my college education. I continued to live with my parents, leaving the mile square that formed Oxford's boundaries only for short trips to visit friends in New York.

So as I prepared to leave for Paris, there was no one to say goodbye. I was frankly relieved to be alone, preferring solitude to the risk of exposing my anxiety and uncertainty. I had to pretend I wasn't afraid to leave.

Once the boat had plowed into the rolling Atlantic, passengers, most of them recent graduates headed for study in Europe, began strolling the deck, introducing themselves to other travelers. With my novel future plans to find a job in Paris, I was besieged by questions about my bold decision to travel alone, with only my small supply of traveler's checks. "But how," "what if" and "when" were the responses to my vague plans. The sudden and unexpected attention made me feel mysterious and daring—qualities that my Midwest would have labeled naïve, or worse, rebellious.

Each day began with breakfast served in the dining room by genial stewards in starched white jackets. By midmorning, the gray decks had been swabbed to a pewter glow and rows of white deck chairs with neatly folded plaid wool blankets were in place. On our first day at sea, the weather was balmy, with smooth, rolling waves under a warm September sun. I joined a crowd of college students who filled the chairs, wrapping their feet in the blankets and sipping steaming cups of hot bouillon served by the deck stewards.

Landfall was eight days away, and each moment added something wondrous and amazing to my life: new friends, interesting young men and always the ongoing romance of travel. The simple comforts of the ship, with time suspended, were better medicine than any antidepressant (though this balm for my malaise had yet to be invented). A mild, miasmic depression had been my constant companion, as much a part of my ambition to be a writer as my rejection slips. The passenger list was overbooked with would-be writers; our shared yearning for worldly experience and attention made for easy friendship and flowing conversation during our long ocean voyage. I was lulled into a delicious state of euphoria, happily confined to my floating world.

I had packed my rejection slips, four from *Seventeen* magazine, a short story market I had tried to crack. The most promising rejection letter had a handwritten note urging me not to give up: "Please try us again. You're almost there." I had also packed my articles, written for the *Miami Student*, the daily campus newspaper. Pat Irving, my favorite French professor, had given me the name of an editor at the *Paris Herald Tribune*. I planned to hand deliver my articles to him. With my new confidence and ease, I began to believe he might offer me a job.

A festive, self-celebratory mood quickly took over and lasted for the entire trip. My days were filled with strolls around the deck, always accompanied by some of the young men on board, and daily games of bridge with a Dutch woman and her two tall, blond sons, who were fluent in English and almost seemed more American than I. Dinner was followed by endless cups of coffee in the lounge or drinks in the bar, and there were movies every night. Our most grandiose plans for living abroad were hailed as brilliant. My life had suddenly gone from aimless despair to giddy anticipation.

On our third day out, the ship was rocked by a strong September storm, typical of the North Atlantic at that time of year. I was trying to read in the ship's library as the boat listed sharply from side to side. Seated nearby were two earnest young women writing their travel diaries, their naive intensity, as I perceived it, making me uncomfortable. I felt a tap on my shoulder and turned to confront an unfamiliar face. A young man. His name was Fred Beck and he casually introduced himself, suggesting that we check the storm's progress on deck. Slightly built with boyish good looks, Fred looked much younger than his thirty-one years. He was a self-proclaimed refugee from the "Madison Avenue rat race," as he described the advertising business. His phrasing was not exactly original but I thought he was terribly clever to denigrate his successful past career. He had recently left his job on a McCann-Erickson account to travel in Europe, his plans as uncertain as mine. We liked each other immediately. I was infatuated with his reflections on my ambitions for independence and freedom, and he accepted the role that I cast him in as my confidant, an older and wiser advisor. I found his reserved and faintly tutorial manner intriguing.

The next morning the weather was again warm, the breeze soft, the sea a large sparkling gem under clear blue skies. I was dozing in my deck chair, feeling particularly blissful, when Fred interrupted my reverie. He insisted that I follow him to the ship's library where he kept a small footlocker. With obvious pride he revealed the contents—a portable typewriter, several new notebooks and a bound book. With mildly sardonic grin, he opened the book and declared, "This is my soon-to-be-famous novel." All the pages were blank.

If I was dubious about Fred's literary talents, he was still a most charming writer manqué and the kind of man I would never have encountered on the Miami campus. His literary ambitions had once been encouraged by Amherst College, his alma mater, and he was going to Paris to write. He confided that his former wife, Marjorie, was a fashion model in Paris. When her girlish gamine face aged, the hard-edged New York fashion world had rejected her. She wisely headed for Paris, where, no longer hampered by her age (still barely more than thirty), she could continue posing for fashion photos and work for couturiers. Marjorie was another reason for Fred's trip. Once I heard that he'd been divorced, he seemed older and less wise.

When Fred left the deck chair next to mine empty, other young men would arrive to take his place. Al, the rusty-blond Jewish boy from the Bronx, became another attentive companion. He loved to discuss literature and history and since he was preternaturally bright and a recent Harvard graduate, his talk was laced with wit and wisdom. He seemed to crave my company, but there was an element missing in his ardor. He once asked me if I was a virgin, and though I hated the question, I admitted that I was. "Oh," he said, "I thought you were a nice girl."

Less talkative but far more handsome was Ian McKelvey, a Canadian Scot with carrot-red hair. He had traveled often to Paris with his mother, though this time he was going alone to study in Provence for a year. He was very concerned about my sketchy plans for living in Paris. He insisted that I needed more than college French to cope with the culture, and that I certainly would need more money. "Oh, no," I assured him. "I have wanted to go to Paris for years. I can't wait until I'm old and rich. And besides, how else can I improve my French?" Though Ian would never have believed it, and I wasn't wise enough to even imagine it, my naiveté would prove to be a kind of protective armor. After all, it was the fifties, a halcyon time for Americans.

A few days into our voyage, Fred, ever alert to literary fame, spotted the name of Katherine Anne Porter on the ship's passenger manifest. Her novel, *Pale Horse, Pale Rider* had established her reputation as a brilliant writer. I had read the book but was mystified by much of the stream-of-consciousness prose. Nevertheless, I was eager to meet her. Our famous writer remained invisible until the final evening of the voyage, when she reluctantly agreed to an informal talk.

I arrived at the standing-room-only event clutching an envelope of my articles and that one letter of encouragement I'd received from *Seventeen*.

The audience was completely absorbed by the delicately pretty Miss Porter. There she was, gray-haired, pale and composed though her hands trembled with nerves, a real writer. Unfortunately, her quiet voice was almost completely drowned out by a raucous storm, its thundering waves crashing against the hull, slapping the windows with walls of water. I had hoped to introduce myself, perhaps even show her my articles. I yearned for advice about writing, but she never returned my gaze, instead she talked earnestly with other young passengers who had more confidence in their literary talent. Were we, I often wondered, an early inspiration for her future novel, *Ship of Fools*?

# Ann Montgomery Will Study At Sorbonne

*MISS MONTGOMERY*    (Photo Courtesy Holland-American Line)

Miss Ann Montgomery, of 2 West Church St., Oxford, posed for photographers on the deck of the Holland-American Liner, "S.S. Ryndam" just before sailing from New York harbor, en route to Paris, France, where she will study French literature at the Sorbonne.

# 2

## Two West Church Street

"My father has bought an old wreck," I told my friends, hoping to fend off the gossip that our shabby new house would create. During World War II, our war, which we innocently referred to as "the war," it was illegal to evict a tenant as long as they paid the rent. But by 1945, the war was over and we were evicted from our rental because the owner wanted to sell. Fortunately, my father had invested in war bonds and he was able to cash those in for a down payment. We looked at lots of houses, my father and I, since my mother was too emotionally distraught to consider the grim houses we could afford. There was one that I liked very much, a bit dark but very comfortable and in a quiet location near the campus. But my father was always worried about money and the price was a bit over our limit. I begged him to take the risk—just once—and buy it, but he refused. Instead he found a house that he could afford, a faded yellow clapboard colonial on the noisy corner of Church and Main. It might have been a proud beauty in 1845, when it was built, but by 1945, the house was in disrepair and showing its age. The rental we were leaving was on a quiet, tree-lined street, one block from the university campus. The new house was across from our gray stone Presbyterian Church, which seemed like a good idea, but from the front porch there was a clear view of the Pure Oil gas station, which made our new location feel slightly disreputable. It was impossible to ignore the traffic noise on Main Street, especially on the hot, humid nights that filled every summer. The small yard was covered with a thin, scrappy crust of patchy grass. There was no privacy planting except for a stunted hedge on one side of the house, nothing to conceal its flaws from the outside world. I was full of adolescent hubris and hated to be so exposed.

Inside the house, the wavy pine floors were covered with several coats of scarred, dun-colored paint. In the living room, the fireplace grate, surrounded by rose-colored Victorian tiles, faced the couch, an antique walnut daybed made by my great-grandfather. Two chairs, a barrel back and a wingback, which my mother had slipcovered in beige and blue, were on either side of fireplace. There were antique oriental rugs over the light blue carpet and ruffled marquisette curtains at the window. My father didn't believe in hiding behind draw draperies. To my adolescent distress, the world had an open view of our first floor from Church Street. When, eventually, all the skeletons fell out of the family closet, there was nothing to hide anyway.

The kitchen, a small addition on the back of the house, had no counters or cabinets and a stained porcelain sink with spindly legs that made it look naked, as if its private parts were exposed. The water pressure in the house was so low that it took half an hour to fill the claw foot tub in the upstairs bathroom. A potbellied stove in the basement had to be stoked with kindling and coal before there was any hot water—and then it only made enough for four or five inches of water. It was not the optimum environment for a fourteen-year-old girl with hair to be washed, socks to keep white and the myriad ablutions that the average teenage life required. In every room the cracked and peeling walls revealed thin lathe and sagging plaster. My mother sobbed in despair the day we moved in. She hated all of it, but she especially hated the floors.

My professorial father was never adept with carpenter's tools or a paintbrush, so my brother and I became the handymen of the house. We painted and painted—furniture, walls, woodwork—but we couldn't do anything about the coal furnace that chugged away all winter only to fill the house with lukewarm air. When I studied late, I sat on the register on the floor of my bedroom and sometimes even wore mittens. But we didn't know what to do about the floors.

By the end of our first summer, we had seeded the yard with grass and planted two dogwood trees that a neighbor had given me. The living room responded kindly to our furniture. It was beginning to feel like a home but, though we didn't know it, our lives would never be the same again.

The move to Church Street broke my mother's thin veneer of stability. Her fragile mental equilibrium began to unravel and within months she was sleepless and tearful, yet often agitated. We had no name for her condition or its cause, and neither did her doctor, a particularly obtuse small town internist. At my father's urging, I accompanied her to a thorough physical with the internist. Beaming confidently at me, he declared her fit and healthy, though he gently accused her of complaining about small aches and pains. Her daily life was confined to household chores, cooking and laundry. She was paralyzed with fear of the small town she knew so well. Her friendships eroded under the stress of her mood fluctuations as her random hostility began to dominate her conversation. She vacillated from frenetic activity to apathy and lethargy.

Years later, our clinical knowledge was broad enough to give us some understanding. After my birth my mother suffered a prolonged episode of fatigue and low spirits that today would qualify as a postpartum depression, but in 1932, there was little understanding of that condition. The recommended cure—three months bed rest—would fail. Psychoactive medication didn't exist. Gradually she appeared to recover some of her former verve and energy, while the farm girl my father hired took over the household. She stayed with our family until I was two. Another episode of depression followed the birth of my brother four years later. My mother was thirty-eight when her last child, my sister, Virginia, was born, and signs of her serious postnatal problems—sleeplessness, crying jags and deadening fatigue—could no longer be ignored. She became temperamental and chronically angry with people and inanimate things like dirty floors, meals to cook and piles of laundry. Her eccentric chatter, laced with paranoid descriptions of imagined enemies, made her a lonely pariah, a role hardly worth playing in a small Ohio town. The decline was gradual and there were periods of normalcy. But by the time my sister was a toddler, my mother's mental stability began to lose out to chaos. Virginia was a cute, bright little girl and wiser than her years; she made frequent attempts to escape the house by running downtown to get hand-outs of candy from the local pharmacist, who loved her visits. My mother would be called and would drop her self-absorption long enough to rush to Main Street to collect her child. Our more-or-less normal family life began to slide into middleclass bedlam.

As the oldest child, I eventually became the custodian of my mother's depression. In the midst of this chaos, we moved to our new house. None of us—my father, my eight-year-old sister nor my fourteen-year-old brother—understood what was happening to her. We understood even less how exhausting it would be to conceal the reality from neighbors and friends as we struggled to care for ourselves. She wandered our world in a haze of hallucinations and babble. My misguided attempts to get support from my friends were rejected as adolescent angst; I quickly learned to hide the reality behind a miserable silence. There is nothing quite so potent as a family secret. Secrecy only intensifies shame and in Oxford, Ohio there was no emotional support for a troubled silence.

My parents met at a cocktail dance in Champagne-Urbana, Illinois, at the home of my father's master's thesis advisor, whose two daughters belonged to my mother's sorority at University of Illinois. It was love at first dance. My father courted my mother from that day until she reluctantly agreed to marry him, the day after Christmas. He had a graduate scholarship to study Classics at the University of Vienna that would begin in January, and he was determined to take her with him to Austria as his wife. She gave up her final semester of college and never did graduate but she and my father had, according to all their stories, a wonderful honeymoon year in Vienna, drinking coffee with heavy cream, beer and white wine and practicing their lifelong waltz. It began, like so many marriages, as a great romance, but reality—the Great Depression, three children and household expenses and, finally, my mother's slow descent into mental illness—took a great toll. I can still hear the strains of Viennese waltzes playing from their small collection of large, heavy records, while, in the best times, they danced together in our living room.

By the time I was in high school, I already longed to escape from my home, with its growing maze of trouble, but even though I dreamed up elaborate travel adventures, I had no way of realizing them. I was lucky enough to have sympathetic teachers as my high school years continued and I developed other interests that distracted me from my mother's lack of composure—performing in high school plays, writing and editing both the school newspaper and the yearbook and making grades good enough to graduate in the top five of my class.

During my senior year, my mother's condition visibly deteriorated and she drifted between periods of relative emotional calm and a highly agitated depressive state. Whenever she closed in on us, we would scatter like feeding birds being chased by a cat, dreading her outbursts of temper. She was a beautiful woman but her appearance became slovenly. She wore the same outfit every day—faded slacks and an old blouse or sweater. Her inexplicable despair created a complex social problem for my father, who had his professorial duties to perform. He tried hard to maintain a symbolic presence of purposeful sanity, laced with a classicist's philosophical wisdom. There was a copy of Freud's essays on top of the refrigerator, but my mother was beyond Freud. My friends came and went in our house, my mother's strange behavior unnoticed, thanks to my father's careful supervision of the chaotic scene that lay behind a calm exterior. Occasionally, my mother would nab a friend's mother on High Street and complain bitterly about my behavior. Then, the woman would explain to me that I had to help my mother more because she was exhausted. I tried to explain that her exhaustion was caused by something besides overwork. But after a few hopeless attempts, I retreated to silence. I was already doing a great deal of the housework that my mother was too weak or too dazed to do.

I hated housework. I wanted to be "alone," writing in my bedroom garret, smoking Camel cigarettes until my head and throat ached. I certainly didn't want to be part of her turmoil, fighting pointless battles against her irrationality. We cautiously watched the shifting dynamics of her affliction, sometimes listening for hours to her sobbing while my father escaped to his campus office. Sometimes we shuddered at her loud cries of anguish and anger, watching her random wanderings through the dark house and yard from our dark rooms. While I was struggling with my own adolescent anguish, I also became her confident and, unintentionally, her victim. Nothing is more agonizing than listening to someone's hallucinatory talk, endlessly repeating phrase after phrase, and pointless story after pointless story, incoherently drifting farther and farther from reality. I was stable enough to know that most of what she said was pure nonsense. But I listened helplessly. What else could I do? She repeatedly said, "I want to die."

There was no cruelty, unless the neglect that accompanies self-absorption is cruel. But there was plenty of despair. Nothing in the small community of Oxford, Ohio prepared me for the unbearable shame and alienation I felt watching the watershed of tears and crushing misery of what was becoming a psychotic depression. In the process, my own dreams and aspirations were put through the shredder of her moods.

I had spent most of my life in Oxford, all of my education since third grade at McGuffey School, a laboratory school established for teacher training by Miami University. McGuffey's red brick building, owned by the university, housed not only kindergarten through twelfth grades but art classrooms for the university. It offered a far better education than the public school in Oxford, and inspired our most creative dreams and ambitions: mine was to become an artist. Yet, by the end of eighth grade, my father countered my enthusiastic plans to attend Pembroke College (then the women's college attached to Brown University, and very near to the Rhode Island School of Design) by explaining that he could not afford to send me away to college, either financially, or as it turned out, psychologically. I was heartbroken and though I didn't give up my dream to go away to college, I could never change his mind. In rebellion, I dropped algebra in ninth grade and though I took science courses, never attended another math class. After two years, I also dropped out of Latin and unlike most of my friends, refused to study French, the only other language that was offered. My father appeared not to notice my self-destructive loss of hope for my academic future. The math teacher tried to change my mind, even offering special tutoring, but I refused his help. My father's decision had defeated my plans and he had won the day. There was nothing I could do but accept Miami University's offer to enter its freshman class in September of 1950. Unfortunately, I was forced, again by my father's claims of financial hard times, to continue living at home. His decision carried more disappointment than I could handle because he had promised me that if I went to Miami, he would let me move on campus to a dormitory. I cried for hours the night he told me that he had changed his mind. He didn't give the real reason but I eventually understood that, without me, he was trapped by my mother's illness. He needed help to manage her and I was the only candidate.

# New York, New York

On New Year's Eve as my first semester of college was ending, I accepted a last-minute invitation to a party from a slightly older group of friends, some already college graduates. That night, I met and fell in love with a young man who was working on his Master's Degree at Northwestern University. It was my first serious love affair. I refused his half-hearted marriage proposal because I was terrified of what I viewed as the "marriage trap." I dreaded the prospect of dutiful domestication. My mother had thoroughly poisoned that well by blaming marriage for her troubles. Yet I was completely infatuated. It was a passionate relationship for me and when it ended, it opened up a chasm of emotional isolation. Living at home with my tormented family isolated me from my classmates, and I dreamed every day of leaving Oxford. Though I was a member of CWEN, the freshman women's honorary, had joined a sorority and was writing for the student newspaper, I saw no purpose to my life or to a college education. I managed to finish the first semester of my sophomore year while making plans for my departure. At the end of my Christmas vacation, I announced to my parents that I was going to New York to get a job. To accomplish this, I had already been helped by a dear friend, a woman two years my senior, who loaned me fifty dollars for the bus fare to New York City. My father, as could be expected, did not approve my plan. But once I had informed the university and my professors that I was leaving, there was no turning back.

When I arrived in the city, my Uncle Kenneth, my father's brother and a managing partner at the then honest Arthur Andersen Accounting firm, met me at Port Authority and took me by taxi to the Parnassus Girls Club on West 110th Street. My father, who initially withheld his support for my escape to New York, had reserved a room for me there. The Parnassus Girls Club was something the world apparently no longer needs, a haven for single young women who were studying at Julliard and living in New York. Because my father was the organizer of Miami University's Artist Series, he had contacts in the music world in New York; one of them had managed to find the room there that I shared with three Julliard students. I had two meals a day and parietal hours ("In by ten, girls!"). With my uncle's help (he sent me to an executive search agency where he was well known), I quickly found a job as the receptionist for the New York City Anti-Crime Committee. I was in the unlikely but safe custody of a group of investigating detectives, all former FBI men. The Anti-Crime committee was established as a nongovernmental organization by the Kefauver Commission to investigate organized crime in New York. My employers were extremely patient as I routinely cut off their important phone calls by mismanaging the switchboard, typed errors into every letter and generally disrupted the tedious routines of the office. I could barely afford the Parnassus Club on my fifty-five-dollar-a-week salary.

After hours, I began to have a wonderful time. I was astounded to discover I could almost always get a single ticket to Broadway plays that everyone told me were sold out. I waited patiently in the standing room ticket line at the Met and saw every opera that season, all produced by the famous impresario Rudolph Bing. I visited museums and also managed to meet my share of eligible and ineligible young men. It was my first experience with an urban world where my appearance turned heads toward me instead of away.

After three months, I was invited to share a shabby, sprawling apartment on the corner of 110th and Broadway with five other young women, all college graduates trying their luck at various jobs in the big city—one as a model and fashion trainee in the garment district, one as a serious classical pianist, one as a lover of musicals who played piano in the pit orchestras, one determined to be a diva with her glorious soprano voice, and one in a fashion-oriented public relations agency. Three of the women were recent college graduates that I had met at Miami. The invitation seemed a great bit of luck since it substantially expanded my freedoms and reduced my fixed expenses. By June, after two of the occupants retreated to their hometowns for the summer, four of us had moved to a summer sublet on East 83rd Street.

My receptionist job was a tedious trap that in the high-adrenaline atmosphere of New York was barely tolerable. Now that I was more or less settled, I decided to expand my search for a new job. What followed was a series of ridiculous fiascos, including one interview where I tried to convince the *New Yorker* magazine to hire me as a researcher. The elderly woman who interviewed me said, "But you haven't even finished college!" After that I answered every classified ad in the New York Times for an "editorial assistant." They all turned out to be from house organs, a particularly bland sector of the publishing industry. I was routinely turned down.

My boyfriend of the moment, Bob Meagher, a law student at Yale, suggested I try modeling. So I did; the Ford Agency set up my first series of trial photos. Elaine Ford thought enough of the results to take me on as part of her highly successful modeling agency.

Everything looked so promising. I imaged that I could earn enough as a model to transfer to Hunter College, shaping my future around staying in New York. But this heady entry into the "real world" wouldn't last. I was heavily asleep one steamy June night when the ringing telephone woke me. My hand holding the phone trembled as my father told me that he wanted me to come home immediately. My mother had been hospitalized with what he hopefully termed a "nervous breakdown." That phone call has remained one of the most frightening experiences of my life. I felt dizzy and nauseated not only from the intense humidity and heat, but also from my father's desperate call. I was haunted by shame and grief. My mother was in a mental hospital, but at that moment, I felt as if she were dead. After brief explanations to my employers at the Anti-Crime Committee and hasty good-byes to my friends and roommates, I packed my suitcase and took the train west. My father, looking weary and anxious, met me in Richmond, Indiana, the closest port to Oxford.

While I had been living in New York far away from family problems, my brother, Henry, and sister, Virginia, aged fourteen and seven, had not been so fortunate. They were there during the last frantic days before our mother was hospitalized—they pursued her down dark streets as she ran, nearly naked, trying to flee her overheated body, and watched over her as she restlessly prowled the house at night. For one week, she didn't sleep at all and when the family doctor finally gave her morphine to induce sleep, three shots had almost no effect. Her broken mind was racing too fast for even the strongest narcotic. As a result (oh, horror of horrors for me, a proper small-town girl), she spent the night in the town jail before a judge's scrutiny would permit my father to admit her to a private psychiatric clinic. Henry, a strong, humorous teenager, stayed with her that night, though her delirium kept her from knowing there was anyone there. Neither of them slept. My father was at home with Virginia, getting some much-needed rest before he would take my mother to the judge's chambers and then to the hospital in Cincinnati, a thirty-mile drive.

After two weeks of shock treatment, the only medicine her doctors had for such a severe depression, she returned home, her health miraculously restored. Two days later she reverted to her manic confusion, just as ill as she had been before hospitalization. Another two-week session followed in the same, extremely expensive private hospital, with more shock treatment. The shock treatments temporarily blocked her memory and she returned after the second hospitalization still weak and dazed. She was calm, but far from well. A few days after my mother was first hospitalized, my brother Henry was rushed to surgery with an emergency appendectomy. In a matter of hours, it seemed, our family was drowning in illness.

The next step was more difficult. My father's brother Kenneth had taken on the expense of the private hospital and shared our confusing turmoil. The psychiatrist's advice, though he had not decided on a diagnosis, was for longer hospitalization. My father and uncle reluctantly agreed that the only recourse was the state hospital. Within days, my mother was admitted to Longview Hospital, a dark, brooding red brick building set high on one of the Cincinnati hills. Its large, sparsely furnished rooms were filled with wandering, jabbering patients. The scene made the hospital in *The Snake Pit*, a movie starring Olivia de Havilland that dealt with mental illness, look like a country club. It held such terror for me that my father had to force me to accompany him on his weekly Sunday visits.

I began my junior year at Miami University with several burdens: sharing the care of my siblings with my father and perhaps more difficult, concealing the nature of my mother's hospitalization from my friends. Mental illness was difficult to treat without the psychoactive drugs available today. Like all seemingly incurable ills, it was not only terrifying, but also, literally, unspeakable. Midway through my mother's stay in Longview's overcrowded wards, psychoactive drugs—in my mother's case, Thorazine—came to the rescue. The wandering, babbling patients suddenly were quiet. Gone were the cold, wet sheet wraps, isolation rooms with padded walls and strait-jackets. Longview began to take on the antiseptic atmosphere of an ordinary hospital, with its heavily tranquilized patients peacefully dozing through the days. Not until the 1980s was my mother correctly diagnosed as a manic-depressive (a term I prefer to bipolar since it more accurately describes the symptoms) and finally treated with lithium. It turned out to be a miracle drug. She would have long periods of health with that medication. But she would never be the person she was before the illness began. At best, she was cautious, anxious and seemingly bewildered by the ravages of mental illness, since she never remembered her psychotic episodes.

An accumulation of extra credits in my freshman and sophomore year that made it possible for the university to give me junior class status, even though I had missed an entire semester of my sophomore year. But, I was an ungrateful scholar and cut almost as many classes as I attended, ignoring reading assignments and cramming for exams to get passing grades. I drifted between dreams of rebellion and waves of my own depression. I wanted someone to validate my anger and to rescue me from my trap. All I accomplished was a lower grade point average.

Whether from nature or nurture, my mother's psychosis was creating a firm conviction in my own mind that I, too, was going crazy. I kept those covert fears to myself until my growing isolation began to create serious problems for me, among them a blossoming case of agoraphobia. Leaving the house was like prying open an oyster and the short walk to the university campus was as torturous as a forced march. I felt, finally, that I could no longer cope and reluctantly (for I did not want to share any of my dark secrets) contacted the student counseling center. The result: an appointment with Dr. Goldstein, a Freudian psychiatrist, Viennese by birth and accent, who came to the campus once a month to evaluate students with symptoms of mental distress and occasionally, mental collapse.

Peering intently at me through glasses as thick as bottle bottoms, he asked me about my life. I wanted to talk about my mother's illness, but he artfully brushed that subject aside, concentrating instead on my responses about my own feelings.

"What do you want to do with your life?" he asked in his strong Austrian accent. "I plan to be a writer," I answered. "Ah, so," he mused. "And can you write?" "I think so," was my tentative reply. "Well," (though he pronounced it "vell"), "then, you will be fine." He ended our session by stating emphatically, "Your mother's problems have nothing to do with you. Forget them and live your own life." I stared at him in disbelief. He hadn't even asked about my inner turmoil—my anxiety attacks, my malaise, my neurosis. His assessment was correct, but I was in no mood to be so abruptly discharged. I wanted to be rescued, not left alone to contemplate how to save myself from myself.

The hard-crusted shell of resentment that protected me from deeper, less acceptable feelings proved to be very hard to crack. I would make no real progress against my black mood until I left home and at that moment, I still had many months ahead of listening to my mother's incoherent ramblings as she drifted in and out of mania. She did not recover fully until the middle of my senior year. Once she was stable, she faced the daunting task of salvaging something of her former life, since her rapidly fluctuating moods had played havoc with the trust of friends and family.

During this period, my father insisted that I accompany her to a recital being given by Jan Pierce, a famous tenor. It was sponsored by the University Artist Series, which my father had helped to launch as part of his determined effort to raise the local cultural level. The recital was my mother's first public event since being hospitalized. She and I found our seats, painfully aware of the furtive glances of people who knew us. I felt hopelessly inadequate to comfort my unusually quiet mother, her hands trembling from embarrassment. Her memory of the past year was vague and she never recalled any of the events of her hostile, paranoid manic periods. Her mind was a blank slate once the shock treatments brought her back to reality. We fixed our eyes on the stage and both of us were deeply relieved when the program began. Because she was a beautiful, artistic and intelligent woman, her defection from reality made her an object of both scorn and pity. To her eternal mystification, the world did not welcome her return. For me, her lack of insight was the most distressing symptom of her illness, though at that stage in my life, my own insight was in short supply.

My graduation from college was a forlorn occasion. I never saw either of my parents, though I think my father had marched in the academic parade with other professors. I walked home, carrying my rented black robe and cap, feeling neglected and abused. How could they completely ignore my hard-won degree? Their explanation was simple enough—they didn't think I cared. Both my father and I privately thought I was failing to realize early promise, or at least, his early assessments of my talents. But even as a failed scholar, I was determined to use my major in French language and literature to go to France. My only goal was to travel. After all, I had really majored in Paris, since I only read half the assignments I was given. It's not surprising that my application for a Fulbright Scholarship was rejected.

Afraid that I would actually carry out my travel plans, my father called a journalist he knew at the Cincinnati *Enquirer* and got me an interview with an editor of the newspaper. If I insisted on my vaunted ambition to be a writer, this, he reasoned, would at least satisfy that desire. By belligerently refusing to attend the interview, I established a precedent—my independence was more important than any job. Cincinnati was simply too close to home. His hopes for a reasonable, secure future for me were destroyed and he logically refused to give me any money for my self-indulgent postgraduate tour of Europe. I was well aware that he also secretly harbored some Victorian ideas about maiden daughters remaining at home to care for their aging parents. Convinced that I would soon be begging him for a safe passage home, he offered only to fund my return ticket.

So I wrote to my Uncle Kenneth, who was more impressed with my ambitious goals than my father. He agreed to pay my boat passage and loan me money to live in Paris until I found work. He believed me when I said I would get a job. In 1954, the value of the dollar on the French exchange was extremely high. With care, I thought that three hundred dollars could last long enough for me to find employment. But I would have to depend on the fact that the xenophobic French were still fascinated by everyone and everything American.

# 4

# Amerluks

We docked at LeHavre on September 26, ten days after leaving New York, and crossed the French countryside by rail, past the partially harvested fields, the farmers in their clogs and blue smocks hocing the ground, the tiny cottages with thatched roofs—a world as quaint as a calendar photo. Would it be a new world of discovery for me? I hoped for the magic moment of self-knowledge, an awakening stirred by novelty. In this placid countryside I could rearrange my thoughts, the very essence of myself, to suit my ambitions. Self-discovery is a process, not a result, I reasoned. My stifling hometown was far away, confined to memory, to make space for the healing anonymity of foreignness. The trim, symmetrical fields, anchored by thatched roof cottages and fieldstone barns, whipped past the windows of my compartment. Centuries of cultivation had transformed pastoral France into a perfectly landscaped countryside. The rugged fields and woods of my midwestern world couldn't compare.

Gare du Nord, our gateway to Paris, was a cavernous glass cathedral. Pale shards of autumn morning sunlight mingled with the smoke of steam engines at rest. The walkway beside the train was teeming with travelers and baggage carriers, the latter grabbing our luggage from the train and sweeping us to the taxi station where dozens of drivers bid for our fares. "*Ici, mademoiselle,*" shouted a short, swarthy man, wearing a black beret and a dark blue smock, the trademark of French manual workers, already hauling my footlocker into the trunk of his cab. "*Vous êtes americaine, oui?*" he said. I didn't realize that everything about me—the turtleneck sweater, pleated plaid skirt and brown penny loafers, the face framed by short bangs—spelled American girl. I nodded and settled into the back seat of his taxi, suddenly unable to speak a word of the language I'd studied for four years.

The taxi took off in a volley of bleating horns and swept along a crowded street lined with open cafés, each dotted with bright blue and green Pernod umbrellas that hovered like birds over the sidewalk. My senses, dulled by the ten days on a gray ocean, were startled by so much color and confusion on the streets. Vespa drivers wove in and out of the traffic like drunks on scooters, accompanied by cars continuously scolding with their blasting horns. The plaintive cries of ambulances and police cars added their soulful song to the frantic pitch of street music. Above the din, Monsieur du Taxi chatted amiably, in an impenetrable tongue, completely unlike the labored sounds we had made in my French conversation class. Like a tourist guide, a proud Parisian unable to resist pointing out the famous landmarks, he gestured to the Arc de Triomphe as we navigated around it like bumper cars in a carnival. We sped down the broad lanes of the Champs-Elysées, neatly trimmed by symmetrical rows of sycamore trees. The avenue opened like a flower onto the place de la Concorde, the Obélisque's marble needle casting its sun-dial shadow on the round plaza elegantly framed by age-darkened stone buildings and graceful arcades. Vivid splashes of orange and gold filled the geometrically shaped beds of autumn chrysanthemums. Paris, in all its extravagant beauty, was about to become my city, at last.

After the sweep of broad boulevards on the Right Bank of the Seine, we sped past the trim gardens of the Tuileries and the magnificent Palais du Louvre, the grand edifice of French royalty before the Revolution, and crossed the Pont Neuf. The narrow, deeply shadowed streets of the Left Bank were dark canyons that formed an impenetrable maze. My driver continued his eager travelogue, pointing to the church of *Saint-Germain-des-Prés* and its secular companion, the *Café Les Deux Magots*. We passed the sturdy buildings of the Sorbonne en route to the beautiful Jardin de Luxembourg in the heart of the Latin Quarter, and swung around the circle of the place du Panthéon. Finally the taxi slowed and moved carefully through the place de la Contrescarpe with its quaint, white globe street lamps rimming a plaza filled with chestnut trees. The tires bumped over the heavy cobblestones of *rue du Cardinal Lemoine*. The driver stopped abruptly at my destination, the *Pension des Grandes Écoles*, Number 75.

The large, faded green wooden doors that blocked the courtyard of the Pension opened slowly when the driver pulled the bell rope. He thrust my suitcase inside and I followed. Three untidy cats perched on the stone walls of the shabby courtyard, stared at me. The pension itself, a stucco structure with peeling white paint and sagging green shutters, intensified my impression that somehow, I must have come to the wrong place. My driver, unburdening himself of my footlocker, assured me that the address was correct. With a final broad smile, he waved away the tip I offered as he retreated to his taxi. I suddenly felt abandoned and wanted to call out, "Wait, don't leave me here." But at the same moment, I felt the thrill of my audacious leap into a foreign world. My familiar patterns had been disrupted, the puzzle pieces shaken. As I stood alone in the courtyard, trembling in the damp, cold air, I realized that a new picture was taking shape.

Except for the cats, the courtyard was deserted. A dank, unpleasant smell—a mixture of cat urine and old rotting mortar and what I would eventually recognize as the smell of bad plumbing—intensified the shock of arrival. Much of Paris was still infected by a war-weary shabbiness that cast a despairing shadow over the grandeur of this ancient city.

When I opened the pension's front door off the small ter- race, the stale smell of the hallway was mixed with the aromas of a meal in preparation. "Hello? Hello?" My greeting went unanswered. Eventually a gray-haired woman appeared, wiping her hands on her smudged white apron, and said something that I could not understand. Her gestures indicated that I should drop my suitcase and, with her encouraging sign language, I found myself heading for the dining room and sitting at one of the long narrow tables.

The pension dining room had four of these long tables, set with white tablecloths and heavy white china for the noon meal. Eventually, small groups of students from the Sorbonne and other guests of the pension began to arrive and take their places at the tables. A few brief greetings and some quiet con- versations between friends barely broke the muffled silence, my first encounter with the deeply ingrained *"vie privée,"* a French reserve that was part of the national character. I remembered my optimistic letter to my uncle: "I will need an inexpensive place to stay. My father thought you might have some ideas."

My uncle's "idea"—the *Pension des Grandes Écoles*—came from his friend, Cabel Greet, then president of Columbia University. The elegant small hotel that exists at the same address today barely resembles the decaying structure of the fifties. But, trusting my uncle's august advice, I had reserved a three-month stay. I was beginning to wonder how I could begin my new life in such dreary surroundings. Over-protected by the naiveté cultivated by my small Ohio town, I felt actual physical discomfort among Europeans; the full psychological impact of foreignness hit me and its liberating qualities were yet to be revealed. I felt suspended, lighter than air, almost as if those heavy, cold winds that sweep through Paris streets could carry me away.

I had already made my first attempts at using the Paris telephone system—in those constricted postwar years still a tangled process of "oui," "non" and "ne quittez pas" while the operator tried to manually complete the call. I was trying to reach Michael Morrisey at the American Embassy, a friend of Leon Irving, my French professor at Miami. Professor Irving had spent the war years in Luxembourg as an Army intelligence officer and had proven to be an invaluable source of Paris contacts, which he willingly shared. The phone at the pension was awkwardly tucked behind a closet door and I had to schedule each call with the concierge. But I did finally reach him and scheduled my first appointment in the search for a job.

Being a foreigner would eventually banish the last vestiges of my young adult depression and replace it with pure bliss.

For the two years that I lived in Paris, I fervently believed that France kept me free of that depression. That was before I discovered that those gray feelings were part of my nature, first arriving when I was barely four and revisiting me when they pleased. In 1992, my doctor, one of several psychiatrists I had consulted over the years, agreed to prescribe the new drug, Prozac (no side effects) that had made the cover of *Newsweek*. It brought slow but longlasting change.

When I left Ohio for Paris, it was to carve a new world, defined by my choices rather than by someone else's necessity. Reverence for the past was discarded, replaced by devotion to the present. From the moment I saw the city, I knew I wanted to be part of it, to devour it and drink it dry.

Sadly, the *Pension des Grandes Écoles*, with its drab and musty atmosphere, was like tea and toast to my palate— definitely not the Paris of my dreams. On my first evening, two Spanish businessmen in their thirties, guests at the hotel, joined me for dinner and afterwards offered to take me to the Lido, a famous Paris nightclub. They exhibited a cavalier charm and though I was a head or more taller than both of them, I accepted the invitation. They insisted that I should not spend my first night in Paris alone. I was introduced to a side of French life I never expected to see—Las Vegas–style chorus girls barely covered in sheer chiffon and feathers and a master of ceremonies cracking jokes (which of course, I couldn't understand). For the finale, a line of the scantily clad dancers performed a boisterous can-can that would have impressed Toulouse-Lautrec. My pallid reaction to their generously conceived evening left my Spanish escorts mystified. While my desire to experience everything French was genuine, it did not extend to the nightclub scene and, determined to pursue more serious entertainment, I made no effort to conceal my disinterest in the Champs-Elysées nightlife.

Two days later, when I was still recovering from a steamship version of jet lag, the inside of my head bobbing even while I brushed my teeth at the small sink in my room, the concierge rapped sharply on my door. The room was so tiny I could barely stand in it and open the door at the same time. A miniature radiator spit inadequate bursts of heat for only an hour or two in the early evening, rattling like a coffin filled with coins. An orange cotton bedspread and matching curtains were poor substitutes for the faded floral chinz interiors I had expected to find. The winter ahead, with ever diminishing funds, was beginning to look grim indeed.

"*Pour vous, mademoiselle, un ami.*" I wasn't expecting anyone but I quickly dressed and went downstairs. The stillness of the pension's courtyard was unbroken except for occasional bursts of loud student laughter. The autumn air was thick with the acrid smell of dead leaves and institutional food. It was a scene which hardly evoked the seductive melodies of Gershwin's "American in Paris," a record I had listened to endlessly during my last summer at home.

There, waiting patiently in the courtyard was Ian McKelvey, my Canadian acquaintance from the Ryndam. "How on earth did you find me?" I asked. Ian, tall and rangy, handsome in a Harris Tweed jacket, was a welcome and reassuring sight. He reminded me that I had given him my address before we left the Ryndam. But he had only come to say goodbye, since he was leaving for Aix-en-Provence the next day to spend a year studying. I had been so lonely since leaving the comfort of shipboard friendships that I nearly wept with disappointment. Without the conviviality of traveling companions on the boat, life suddenly seemed very bland. "I wish I were going to Aix," I said, imagining the comfort of carefree student life in a small city. "I can't bear to spend another day in this dismal pension!" As I repeated my litany of complaints, Ian listened thoughtfully. My room was too small and even the bedsheets were cold and damp, the French students were unfriendly, the *bonne femme cuisine* unimaginative. "My mother has an old friend, Madame Biguet," he interrupted. "She owns a charming hotel on the rue des Beaux Arts. There are two rooms on the top floor that she sometimes rents to students. Let's go there and talk to her." I ran to my room to get my black coat and we walked quickly out of the courtyard, closing the heavy wooden doors behind us.

An invitation to walk through the streets of Paris was always like an invitation to waltz—irresistible. We turned right on rue du Cardinal Lemoine, a shadowed canyon lined by rows of nineteenth-century white stucco townhouses, their decorative wrought-iron balconies leaning precariously over the sidewalks. At the bottom of the hill, we turned onto rue des Écoles and the jumble of Paris traffic resumed—taxi drivers rudely jostling private cars out of their way, always in a hurry to reach their destination. Conversation was impossible as we neared boulevard Saint-Michel, where buses and trucks and roaring motorbikes joined the car traffic. My unpracticed ear strained to understand the avalanche of French words. After boulevard Saint-Germain, we turned with relief onto the relative quiet of rue de Seine where a first-class outdoor market of fresh food ruled the street and cars were forbidden. I explained to Ian that, in three days, my savings had already been dramatically reduced—three hundred dollars, intended to last three months until I found a job, had shrunk to two hundred and fifty. I realized that life in this seductive city could easily exceed my small daily budget and that it would be hard to find a room as inexpensive as the one at the pension. I felt trapped again by the same circumstances that had kept me in Oxford, Ohio. I would need money to support my expatriate life—more money than I had borrowed—and the thought filled me with an all-too-familiar despair.

Madame Biguet's Hotel de Nice on the rue des Beaux Arts was comfortably settled in the heart of Saint-Germain-des-Prés. Saint-Germain was then as now the arrondissement of the famous cafés, Les Deux Magots, Brasserie Lipp and Le Café Flore, watering holes for idle tourists, expatriates and the rich and famous who gave them their exalted reputations. But it had once been the center of a large monastic community where, until the French Revolution banished them, nuns and priests lived in small medieval houses clustered around the church of Saint-Germain-des-Prés. The famous L'Université de Paris, la Sorbonne, was across the boulevard in the Latin Quarter, the two *quartiers* forming a seamless district that attracted those who preferred the lively ambiance of the Left Bank to the broad formal boulevards of the Right Bank, always empty after business hours.

The Hotel de Nice, a former *hotel particulier*—the French term for an elegant Parisian townhouse—had a quiet location on rue des Beaux Arts, a street just one block long, between rue de Seine and rue Bonaparte. At one end, on rue Bonaparte, was the Ecole des Beaux Arts, the famous French art school partially hidden behind an imposing wall of high black iron fencing. At the other end was the Academie Raymond Duncan. Raymond Duncan, the brother of the famous dancer and bohemian Isadora Duncan, was best known for his eccentric habit of wearing a white toga whenever he appeared. An artist manqué, he claimed to be a painter but actually lived off his deceased sister's fame and whatever money she had left behind. On the top floor of the academie, the American Ollie Harrington, a black writer and habitué of Left Bank cafés, hosted a movable feast in his apartment, an endless party for expatriate writers and the inevitable crowd of hangers-on, serving his famous apple pie with suitable libations.

As we turned off the rue de Seine onto rue des Beaux Arts, we passed an elegant art gallery featuring lithographs by Toulouse-Lautrec. Across the street from the Hotel de Nice was the shabby Hotel des Beaux Arts where Oscar Wilde died. In another three decades, it would become, like the rue des Beaux Arts itself, very fashionable and expensive, standing aloof, the only hotel on a street of art galleries. But in 1954 it was a modest and charming place, in the heart of the Left Bank, where even a writer down on his luck could afford to live and die. Ever the ironist, Wilde himself wrote, "when good Americans die, they go to Paris."

We entered the Hotel de Nice through a heavy glass door, encrusted with elaborate scrolls of black iron grillwork. The reception and living rooms were carpeted in the plush renaissance wine velvet carpet that the French loved so much. There were cozy arrangements of soft, overstuffed couches flanked by trim Louis Quatorze chairs. Bouquets of fresh flowers nested on the coffee tables. Beside the reception desk was a tiny elevator with glass sides and sparkling brass trim that made it look like a birdcage. A pleasant hum would accompany its slow rise through the open iron grill frame to floors above. The Hotel de Nice was as comforting and serene as my pension was dark and brooding.

Ian asked me to wait while he talked to Madame Biguet, who was stationed behind the reception desk. She stood calmly, listening to Ian (a completely bilingual Canadian), cautiously peering over his shoulder at me. Finally she asked to speak to me. I was subjected to her bourgeois grilling; a series of questions intended to separate the proper from the improper. She was slightly suspicious of me. *"Pourquoi etes vous à Paris, mademoiselle?"* I explained that I was a French major in college (*"Ou?"*), *"l'University de Miami, a l'Ohio."* *"Mais ou habitent vos parents?"* *"A l'Ohio. Mon père est professeur."* Though I found it difficult to explain myself in her language, Madame Biguet pressed hard for the information that she was seeking. I persevered because I loved the atmosphere of the hotel and wanted to stay. Her reservation, according to Ian, was that I was not really a student, nor was I employed. I managed to convince her that I had enough backing for three months' residence while I looked for a job.

Madame Biguet turned out to be, in her matronly way, every bit as generous as Ian said she was. She arranged for me to rent a small garret room on the top floor of the hotel with breakfast and dinner for the same amount of money I was spending at my Left Bank pension. My garret had a casement window looking out over the rooftops of *Saint-Germain-des-Prés*, a generous armoire, a small dresser and a bed piled high with a goosedown duvet. Here, at last, was charm, even if on a small scale. The Paris of my dreams was back.

The hotel itself was gift enough, but I was to discover that its cuisine was the real attraction. The menu prepared by Madame Biguet's chef was utterly delicious—savory stews, perfectly prepared *grillades*, steak with *pommes frites*, and the freshest of salads and fruit. I will never forget my first taste of a Bosc pear. The brown color looked unappetizing but the plain skin concealed a gourmet treat, both tart and sweet. The best food of France and Algeria (the source of fresh fruits and vegetables all winter) was still shipped to a central Parisian market, the justly famous Les Halles. It provided the French with quite simply the best food in Europe. Such exquisite fare, when prepared by Parisian chefs, made dining out, and in the Hotel de Nice, one of the great pleasures of my life in that city.

As soon as Madame Biguet and I had finished our discussion about the room, Ian and I went off for a celebratory lunch at the Restaurant des Beaux Arts on the corner of rue Bonaparte, a delightful family restaurant that was a great favorite of left bank expatriates and students. By the time I became a habitue of the Left Bank myself, I would know the regulars at the Beaux Arts, a group of artists and writers more infamous than famous—except for the English poet Christopher Logue, a thin, nervous young man who eventually became well known in his native land. In the spring, I would introduce two young men to the Beaux Arts—Charles Brower, the brother of my future husband, and William Vanden Heuvel, an acquaintance from New York who was passing through Paris en route to Southeast Asia. This was the period when the French were losing their battle to keep Viet Nam as a colony. Though it was not general knowledge, the Americans were beginning to contribute their financial and military aid. Bill Vanden Heuvel proudly announced that he was going there to serve under a General Bill Donovan, a famous, tough American who was in charge of covert operations in, unbelievably, Viet Nam. Americans might have been shocked to hear of their country's involvement as early as the summer of 1955.

The Beaux Arts, with its bohemian atmosphere, was always on my tour of the Left Bank for newcomers to the city. By the entrance, there was a set of open boxes where nineteenth century art students once kept their cloth napkins. The restaurant's menu specialized in simple provincial cooking at bargain prices—*sauté de boeuf bourguignon* and *classic coq au vin*—delicious fare for the artists and writers who found it so appealing.

Ian was the kind of young man I would meet frequently during my stay in Paris—attracted to me by my appearance, attractive to me for his deferential manner. He had his own extraordinary good looks and a gentle intelligence. He was eagerly anticipating his year of study in Aix-en-Provence. I knew little about him except that he lived in Montreal and had graduated from McGill. He said he planned to go to law school after his year in France. His brief references to his family made them sound prosperous, and it was clear that his mother exercised a strong influence on him. She was a Francophile who had lived in Paris as a young woman. His father was the typical scion of the upper middle class—hardworking, driven to succeed and rarely at home. His shadowy figure created a family structure the opposite of mine, where my father was the nurturing parent and my mother withdrawn and self-absorbed. I had no solid financial support and I couldn't survive the background checks from these handsome admirers of mine. Nor could I honestly pretend to aspire to the calm, secure futures they envisioned for themselves.

More important, though, arriving as he did unannounced when my initial euphoria about Paris had been eclipsed by expatriate angst, Ian was quickly elevated to the role of my rescuer. When he introduced me to Madame Biguet and the Hotel de Nice, I was so grateful for his help that I couldn't help being a little in love with him. He had given my life a new direction that I would never have found alone. But after he left Paris, I never saw him again.

The next day, I moved into the Hotel de Nice. Walking up the winding staircase of the hotel, I almost collided with two small blond children, half walking, half tumbling down. Behind them, their mother greeted me warmly with a wonderful broad smile and introduced herself as Holly Massee, saying she remembered me from the Ryndam. I had never noticed the Massees, a handsome young American family from Prairie Village, Kansas, traveling in cabin class. But they had noticed me. Holly later told me, after we became friends in Paris, how amusing she and her husband, Jack, had found it to watch so many different young men accompany me around the ship.

Jack was a freelance journalist, disappointed in a stalled career that had consisted mainly of articles for a community newspaper. He and Holly were seeking a new venue. Backed by her trust fund, they had chosen Paris, the mythic Mecca for American writers. Holly's maiden name was Hoover. Decades later, a former Smith classmate of hers would explain to me that Holly's name and the trust fund came from the manufacture of vacuum cleaners.

It was the ideal moment to meet Holly. Her wanderlust fired by a year of study in Paris while she had been at Smith College, she had a prodigious appetite for *la bonne vie*. Once she became a Parisian expatriate, she mastered the art of French cuisine, effortlessly turning out such gourmet treats as perfect *oeuf en gelé* molded in her American muffin tin and garlicky mouthwatering stews from the cheapest cuts of meat. With no thought of looking for a job and far more disposable income than I had, she could devour the cultural delicacies of and become a connoisseur of French intellectual life. When I first knew her, her capacity for independent thought and her liberal politics were a bit beyond me; what struck me as terribly daring seemed almost mundane to her.

The chance encounter in the Hotel de Nice was the beginning of a lifelong friendship. We immediately sat down in the living room to discuss the two weeks that had elapsed since our arrival. Somehow the fame of Madame Biguet's excellent kitchen had spread as far as Kansas City and Holly and her husband Jack, a writer, and their two children, four-year-old Robin and two-year-old Mike, were living in a suite on the second floor while they looked for a suitable apartment. It was no easy task in a Paris still cramped from wartime deprivation, to find a place to live. They too had the two meals a day that accompanied the rooms, though I never dared ask what it cost them, nor did I reveal how little I was paying. When Holly left for the Jardin de Luxembourg, a child clasping each hand, we promised to get together for dinner that night.

Several months after we became friends, she called, her voice edgy with urgency, and asked me to meet her in the Jardin des Tuileries. As we sat on a stone bench in the spring sunshine, she explained that she had fallen in love with a wonderful Frenchman and was seriously contemplating a liaison with him. I was flattered to be taken into the confidence of this worldly woman, five years older than I, but I remained silent, uncertain of an adequate response. She repeated frequently during our conversation, "If anyone had ever told me that this could happen to me, I would have been shocked and hurt." I didn't feel wise enough or sophisticated enough to deal with my own life, let alone hers. Though I'm certain it had no effect on the outcome, I was prudish enough to discourage her from pursuing a romance with the—of course—married Frenchman. She decided on her own to remain the constant wife.

The first few weeks of my stay in Paris were devoted to a bewildering and exhausting search for employment. Setting up appointments on the archaic telephones was followed by the complexities of navigating the bus and Metro system. Although I had read French literature, I could not read a French menu. Every penny, or in this case, every franc I spent had to be carefully accounted for. Without the comforts of Madame Biguet's hotel, my first months in Paris would have taken on quite a different cast. The dual pleasures of excellent food and a warm garret room made everything possible.

Matthew Morrisey, Professor Irving's friend who worked at the U.S. embassy, finally returned my call. I went to his office, where he explained that there were formidable barriers to finding a job with an American government agency. The security clearance, a costly and elaborate ritual of FBI checks and counterchecks, was almost never processed for someone already living abroad, so looking for work in the American sector was hopeless. But rather than set me adrift in a foreign city, he cushioned the shock of the gloomy scenario: the Minister of Siam had recently called him, looking for someone to help him improve his English, since he anticipated being posted to

Washington. Mr. Morrisey suggested that I would be the ideal candidate and I agreed, thankful to have at least one job interview on the horizon. When I left the embassy, I immediately made an appointment with the minister.

The Siamese embassy was in an elegant stone mansion overlooking a park on the Right Bank of the Seine. As I entered his office at the appointed time, the minister rose to greet me with a handshake, a gracious gesture that preceded any meeting in Paris and was still a novelty to me. In America, in the fifties, women held hands with men but only rarely did they shake hands. He stood, drawing himself to his full height of approximately five feet five inches. A wide, burled wood desk with gilt trim separated us and he gestured toward a tapestry-covered chair, asking me to sit. He seemed delighted to see me and I found myself agreeing to meet with him three mornings a week to read and discuss the *Paris Herald Tribune* (my idea). Then he said, "And tonight we will have dinner at the Tour d'Argent. My driver will pick you up at seven." How French—with a Siamese accent! A social invitation with this strangely eager older man was anything but welcome. If I was almost twice his height, he was almost twice my age. I said I was busy, trying to make it clear I wouldn't accept. "Tomorrow night then," he persisted. I shook my head and backing out of the room, bumped into the office door with a painful thump, then turned and ran out of the ministry. Chagrined by my clumsy exit, I was still shaking when a taxi stopped to return me to my safe haven at the Hotel de Nice.

Shortly after arriving in Paris, I had gone to the offices of the *Paris Herald Tribune* to deliver copies of articles I had written for my college newspaper, the *Miami Student*, to Tom

Brunswick, an editor at the newspaper and another close friend of Professor Irvin's. His secretary took the material and promised he would call, but two weeks had elapsed without any word from him. Steeling myself for rejection, I telephoned for an appointment. Finally, he agreed to see me.

As I watched my funds shrink, I was growing more anxious about finding work, and every interview became an ordeal. I had to face my own deep fears of rejection at the same time that I was forced to assert myself in spite of bouts of timidity and lapses of self-esteem. There were many days when I had to force myself to the telephone and then drag myself to each appointment. But the consequences of failure outweighed my worst anxieties. Somehow, I would find the energy to make each new appointment and then find the resolve to follow through.

All this made me utterly miserable, burdened with dreadful, nameless fears that I knew I could not reveal to anyone. One of the things you learn growing up in a small town is that once strong emotions are expressed, out of the closet, they take on a haunting life of their own. I feared that the dark stain of squandered confidences would stick to me like a shadow. Better not to be truthful, not to indulge in complete candor. Yet it took great effort for me to conceal my emotions. My parents' admonishments to "exercise self-control" were wasted on me. My feelings, much too intense, were always pressing for expression. Attempting to hide them was as hard as trying not to breathe. My emotional misery leaked out like battery acid, sending people I hoped to charm running away, unable to endure my despair. I had an acute need for self-exposure, as if only what I could reveal had any reality for me. "Do you really feel that bad?" my incredulous friends would ask. As for my doomed relationship with my mother, no one offered sympathy, or even understanding.

When my mother complained about me, as she frequently did to anyone who would listen, they in turn criticized me. It was always my fault. My friends agreed that I was at fault. Their mothers loved them—unconditionally. Until I was well beyond middle age, I kept silent about my mother's illness. I was more afraid of speaking openly about it than I was of the illness itself. To form relationships, however, I had to learn to pretend to candor, so I invented a new persona who was less inhibited. I began to accept some emotional misery as natural to my newly independent status, and I learned to endure the pain—even to ignore it. There was no time in my new life for self-indulgent introspection. I was surrounded and inspired by new experiences. It was in Paris that I became a deep believer in taking action to effect a cure.

As I was ushered into the office of the *Paris Herald Tribune,* I felt triumphant. It was exactly where I wanted to be, I believed, as I looked at the rows of desks loaded with typewriters and paper, and heard the teletype machine ticking as it rolled out the latest news. Mr. Brunswick looked the competent editor he was, reading glasses shoved down on his nose as he solemnly regarded me. He was definitely serious, though his questions to me indicated that he didn't think I was. I was always mysti-fied and hurt if I was dismissed as a frivolous lightweight. His scrutiny of me (he had read my articles) was unnerving. When he said he had been impressed with my writing, I felt cautiously hopeful. "Do you really want to work for a newspaper?" he asked. I expressed my heartfelt desire to work for the *Herald*

*Tribune*, emphasizing that I was committed to staying in Paris and that my goal was to become a journalist.

With considerable sympathy, he said, "I would like to encourage you since you obviously can write, but there's nothing I can offer now. We are simply not hiring any reporters." Though I took some comfort from the fact that I had been defeated by circumstances beyond my control, I was deeply disappointed. He at least offered to keep my articles and my phone number, adding, "Perhaps something will turn up—and good luck."

My final job interview was held one week later and involved a long train trip to the suburbs of Paris. Holly told me that in her search for schools for her children, she had been to a bilingual nursery school in Saint-Cloud. They had asked her if she was interested in teaching. She declined the offer, but since I had enlisted everyone's help in my search for work, she suggested I pursue the possibility.

What a drab institution it was, with a stern headmistress who reacted to my every response with disapproval. She asked if I too was a Smith College graduate. Did I know anything about children? Asking myself why I was there, I confided that the only experience I had for the job was a tenuous grasp of conversational French and fluent English. I could certainly communicate with three-year-old children in both languages. "I'm afraid," she said without apology, "we need someone who speaks English with a British accent." That was only one of the things I lacked. I headed back to Paris with no regrets.

Without a work permit, an American could not be hired. It was a classic "Catch 22"—you could not get a work permit from the French government without a job and you could not get a job without a work permit. Without proof of employment, you could not become a permanent resident of France. Foreigners were forced to leave the country every three months to renew their *carte de séjour* in order to remain in Paris. I was now confronting the very real possibility that, like many other expatriates, I would never find work. But I could not, would not, even consider returning to Ohio.

One late November evening, I entered the lobby of the Hotel de Nice to be greeted by loud, angry voices. A serious disagreement was under way in French and English. A dark-haired American man spotted me through his horn rims and said, "Can you help us? I don't speak a word of French!" He introduced himself as Linley Stafford, a writer (yet another one). I agreed reluctantly to employ my limited bilingual skills. Madame Biguet was playing the role of *force majeure*, her lightly corseted round form providing impressive ballast. Lin and his wife, Barbara, an equally well-rounded woman with a handsome head of auburn hair, were in a towering rage. I agreed to help, with some misgivings about my competence to represent their case to Madame Biguet. The cause of the dispute: A bottle of wine, chilling on the window ledge of the second floor suite, had fallen to the street (or been thrown) and smashed the windshield of the Staffords' black Renault *quatre chevaux*. Unfortunately, the residents of the suite, the Humphreys, had only just arrived in Paris. Mr. Humphrey was the new president of the Paris office of J. Walter Thompson, the New York advertising agency. He and his beautiful wife and their three handsome children were the jewels in Madame Biguet's crown, and she was adamantly refusing to take them to task as the guilty party. The Humphreys were living at the de Nice while their right bank apartment was being remodeled.

In the middle of the discussion—I trying my best to diplo-
matically translate the Staffords' angry dialogue, and Madame
Biguet resisting any call to action—a gendarme someone had
called arrived from the *Saint-Germain-des-Prés* préfecture. After
examining the damage to the car, his only action was to issue
a ticket to the Staffords for parking on the wrong side of the
street, referring to a regulation that had never been enforced on
the rue des Beaux Arts. At this point, Lin and Barbara started
to laugh, and the absurdities of Parisian life carried the day.

When finally confronted with the story the next day, the
Humphreys were happy to sign insurance papers. The damage
to the Renault was paid. The Staffords, in gratitude, took
me out for a multicourse meal and we became friends. I had
learned I could express myself in French—now I had to learn to
understand it. The argot for the young Americans that flooded
the Left Bank of Paris in the fifties was Amerluks, "lucky
Americans." I would have to become an Amerluk in this city,
so blessed with beauty and the good life that my bleak beginning would eventually seem like a bad dream. But I could not
continue to rely solely on pure luck. I would have to learn the
first lesson in the primer of Paris life: *Il faut toujours se battre*,
you must always fight for yourself. I understood that being an
expatriate in Paris was not an original act. But determined not
to look back, I decided that I was.

I shared the sixth floor of the hotel with Nicole, a beautiful,
petite blond French girl who was studying at the École des Beaux
Arts. She had a large room at the end of the hall, the only other
space, filled with her charcoal drawings and oil canvases. Every
time we met it seemed she was either sobbing uncontrollably,
her large blue eyes rimmed with melting mascara, or wiping

away the tears. Something in her life was causing a lot of distress and I eventually learned it was her boyfriend, also an art student. Her parents knew nothing of their relationship and she was very secretive about it. Once I asked her what was wrong, why she was crying, and she gave a typical French reply: "*C'est rien.*" It's nothing.

Holly had befriended her, trying to help with her endless bouts of depression, and Nicole had confessed to her that she was pregnant. A back-alley abortion was her solution to this dilemma and afterwards, her life would briefly return to normal until the next abortion was needed. (France was a Catholic country that didn't permit contraception.) Holly tried to reason with Nicole, begging her to go to London where she could get a diaphragm, but she adamantly refused. Her self-destructive behavior seemed to me almost a cry for attention. Her boyfriend always looked, understandably, very grim. Once he graduated, they finally got married, but Nicole continued her risky method of birth control and at twenty-one died of septicemia, the result of a final abortion.

Since I was two years older than Nicole and not even close to facing such enormous adult problems, I was both shocked and annoyed by her behavior. But, I was still learning how vulnerable women were to the protestations of the opposite sex, to say nothing of the persuasive powers of arousal.

# 5

# Another Me

It was early afternoon on the last Sunday of October and the hazy autumn sun was casting a thin veil of light over the city. It was the kind of day when even the hardiest expatriates felt a touch of *mal du pays*. For weeks Fred Beck had tried unsuccessfully to phone me at the *Pension des Etudiants*. Now settled in his own Left Bank hotel, he had finally discovered, through a chance meeting with Jack Massee, that I was staying at the Hotel de Nice. Jack and Fred had gone to college together at Amherst.

When the reception desk rang the small intercom outside my room I was surprised to hear that I had visitors. I walked downstairs to the lobby and was stunned to see Fred waiting for me with two companions—his former wife, Marjorie, and her companion, Christopher Perret, a young French-American poet. After the ritual handshake and two kisses, one on each cheek, the continental greeting I had quickly adopted from the French, introductions were made. Marjorie had an intriguing, watchful manner that made her seem distant; Christopher was her smiling but equally inscrutable partner. The weather was still warm so we headed for a walk along the Seine. Boxy, roofed stalls of books, paintings and drawings lined the crowded *quais* on the banks of the river. While Christopher and Fred thumbed through the stacks of prints and lithographs, hoping to find a bargain, I described my life to Marjorie. I told her my search for work had been a series of fiascoes with no results. The comic interview with the overly eager Minister of Siam had canceled my plan to teach him English, and the bilingual nursery in Saint-Cloud didn't like my American accent. The most promising interview, at the *Paris Herald Tribune*, had inconclusive results.

Four years before, Marjorie, at age thirty, already too old for the fast-paced, youth-oriented New York fashion scene, had moved to Paris. Her gamine look—short blond hair with a side sweep of bangs framing her large brown eyes and perfect high cheekbones—was popular with the French. She worked successfully as a photographer's model and, after Chanel asked her to present the 1954 collection, settled into relative economic security as one of the famous couturier's models. She seemed ageless, and I looked at her with fascination—a real model that could transform herself into the perfect fashion image I had so often studied in magazines.

Though Coco Chanel had closed her internationally known *maison de couture* during World War II, her prestigious salon de parfum on rue Cambon stayed open. German officers provided a ready market for her famous perfume, Chanel No. 5. When Coco's first post-war collection appeared, in February 1954, she was seventy years old, but still at the height of her creative powers. Her collection heralded the reopening of Chanel's, in spite of the fact that the fashion press labeled it a "melancholy retrospective" and "a fiasco." Only the March 1, 1955 issue of American *Vogue* had a positive comment, "…if the simplicity of her line is not new…its influence is unmistakable." It was that very simplicity that would eventually triumph over the opulent New Look created by Dior and the splendor of collections by Balenciaga, Balmain and Jacques Fath.

I had ninety dollars left in my armoire at the Hotel de Nice—my bank of choice since foreigners were not permitted to open accounts in French banks. That ninety dollars had become a symbol of my defiance. I would refer to it often in the weeks ahead when I described how close I came to being penniless. Where was my luck? I wondered, convinced by now that all lives were controlled by chance.

As Marjorie and I spoke, the Seine flowed by placidly, its green waters streaked with pale blue reflections of the sky, flotillas of fallen leaves pushing against the stone banks. A *bateau mouche* filled with tourists appeared at the curve of the river and I could hear accordion music and laughter. I had never loved Paris more than I did at that moment.

Fred looked at Marjorie inquiringly. "What about Chanel?" And turning to me, he asked, "What about modeling?" Marjorie hastily explained that Chanel's *maison de couture* had yet to regain its former eminence. There were already too many *mannequins*, she said. She was not about to share her influence at Chanel with me, but she did mention, grudgingly, the name of a photographer I might call.

As the sun disappeared behind Notre Dame, Christopher bought a bottle of red wine and we adjourned to Marjorie's apartment on the Île de la Cité. The apartment was charming, part of a former *hotel particulier*, with high, carved plaster ceilings, beautiful moldings and large windows that looked out on the Seine.

Because Christopher's French father and American mother both lived, separately, in Paris, he was the one among us who could navigate most easily in both cultures. Though he wrote exclusively in English, he was completely bilingual. In a few months, he and Marjorie would marry (an ill-advised move for both of them), but at that moment he was free. He had an elfin charm and a way with women probably inherited from his father. And he was pure poet—a romantic daydreamer. I found him irresistible. Among other things, he could always get medicine at the pharmacy, and for this he proved invaluable. Prescription strength drugs were easily obtained if you knew how to ask. He could provide antidotes for a variety of expatriate ills, particularly gastrointestinal "crises " caused by the foreign bacteria we freely ingested with our food. On more than one occasion, I had to enlist his help.

In the companionable atmosphere of her apartment, Marjorie agreed at last to consider my future as a fashion model, thoughtfully appraising my face and features. Would I pass inspection? I wondered.

"I think you could be a model," she said, almost as if she were handing down a sentence. To emphasize her approval, she lifted a zipper bag of makeup from her purse, announcing that she would teach me the essentials of a "camera-ready" face. She held a small red compact of Maybelline dark black mascara. Using a thin artist's paintbrush moistened with water, she first outlined my eyes by dipping the brush into the cake of mascara, as if it were a pot of black paint. With a few quick sketch marks using a dark brown makeup pencil, she arched and emphasized my eyebrows. French fashion chic at that moment dictated that eyebrows be drawn longer, stretching into exaggerated arcs. To further accentuate my eyes, a modish almond shape was heavily outlined in black. The combined effect made me look like a frightened fawn. Bright pink lipstick, applied with another small brush, was thinly outlined with a deep wine colored pencil. Blue-gray eye shadow colored the space above my eyelids and powdered rouge, applied with a soft brush, sculpted my cheeks. I stared at my altered reflection in the ornately framed mirror above the fireplace. Large, luminous blue eyes dominated my thin face. I thought I looked as aloof and seductive as an Egyptian princess. My romance with the mirror had begun.

"You're beautiful! Beautiful!" explained Fred, applauding as if I were already in the limelight. "Another you!"

Marjorie made the phone call to the fashion photographer she had vaguely mentioned during our walk. I wrote his address on a scrap of paper: 153 boulevard Haussmann. George Saad, the photographer for the French fashion magazine *L'Art et La Mode,* had agreed to see me.

The next morning, I reached into the bottom of my armoire and pulled out some of my precious francs for a taxi to the photographer's studio. Opening the black fake leather folder that held my traveler's checks, I looked at my last twenty-dollar check and, with a sigh, returned it to the armoire.

To me the grand, stone-carved buildings and glittering shops of the Right Bank looked intimidating. But the elegant facades turned out to be just another disguise for the same musty, ancient interiors found everywhere in postwar Paris. The electric lights of the hallway, meant to illuminate the way to the studio, turned off automatically seconds after the button was pushed, leaving me suddenly plunged into darkness. I was trembling with anxiety as I walked up the narrow, sloping, now-dark stairway to the second floor studio.

George Saad was seated at a small desk, wearing a dark green beret, shrouded in a fog of acrid, pungent smoke, his blue packet of Gauloise cigarettes in his hand. A single light that hung from the ceiling dimly lit the room. I introduced myself in my best college French: *"Je suis une modèle Americaine."* *"Ah, oui, mademoiselle,"* he replied, *"Vous êtes un mannequin Americain?"* he said, substituting the correct French word and phrasing for my clumsy literal translation from English to French. The word *"modèle,"* I discovered, referred only to those women who posed nude for painters.

The French have an admirable determination to teach foreigners to speak their language with precision. The method of instruction is simple. The foreigner, the pupil, says something in French. The French instructor (a taxi driver, a tabac clerk) repeats the phrase, correcting grammar, vocabulary and accent. This process made for many painfully slow conversations for me. Everything had to be said three times, since the pupil was expected to repeat the corrected version before conversation could continue. *"Oui,"* I repeated, correcting my vocabulary, *"Je suis un mannequin Americain."* The lesson terminated, M. Saad asked to see my pictures.

"I left my photographs in New York," I said, certain my white lie would be uncovered. To my amazement, he accepted this excuse for not producing the portfolio I didn't have. Scrutinizing my face in the dusky light, he asked me to return the next day at ten o'clock. In less than ten minutes, the meeting was over.

As simple as that! Test photos in the morning. Before our celebratory dinner that evening, Fred and I went to an oyster bar since he could not believe I had never eaten raw oysters. He orchestrated the order for three varieties of fresh ones. The oysters arrived, beige, pale green and blue, glistening in their craggy shells. We ate them with small slices of dark rye bread, flavored with a squeeze of lemon juice, followed by a sip of dry white wine. We had dinner at a small bistro on the rue Saint-Jacques. With more encouragement from Fred, I ordered escargots, snails that arrived in their shells, swimming in butter and garlic. This was followed by *truite meuniere*, delicately sautéed with toasted slivers of almonds. The waiter then brought a whole fish, the eyes and scales shiny and slick, looking as if it had just been caught. I had no idea how to approach this bit of French cuisine, since fish at my family's midwestern table was always a frozen fillet. The attentive waiter solved the problem. Using my knife, he cut across the fish, under the head, then down the middle. Once he'd created the opening, he pulled out the spine, each tiny vertebra completely intact. He smiled, proud to have displayed French *savoir-faire* to the uninitiated foreigner. *Truite meuniere aux amandes* became a favorite dish and I could soon fillet a fish as deftly as any waiter.

Those test photos were never taken. When I arrived at M. Saad's studio the next morning, an impeccably dressed man, tall and trim, holding a king's ransom of mink and fox furs, was introduced to me as the client, an executive from Revillon Furs. Seconds later, I was ushered into the tiny dressing room by Guy, Saad's assistant, the young Swiss who would help me prepare for the photography session. I had carefully applied my makeup, following Marjorie's tutorial, before leaving the hotel. Guy looked closely at my face, added more eye shadow and pulled my short hair into a tiny bun, covering it with a silk chignon cap. I watched the proceedings, suddenly inarticulate, frozen before the mirror. He dressed me in a floor length, luxurious mink coat and before I had a chance to worry about my inexperience, I was under the strobe lights and following Saad's cryptic instructions: "Lower your head. Eyes to the camera, face left, right." Good angle. Click, click.

The fashion world was as capricious then as it is now. It seemed as though attention and flattery were freely given if you made no effort at all and, conversely, all the effort in the world might not produce a single encouraging word. M. Saad was not a talkative photographer, giving more time and attention to the lighting than to me. He disappeared completely under a black cloth that covered both his head and the top of the camera. Occasionally, after a long interval of staring into the camera, he would ask me to change the pose or direct my gaze to another corner of the room—"*Regardez la.*" Every few minutes he would shout at his assistant to adjust the lighting. The tricks of the trade—safety pins and clothespins that held a garment in place, bare feet under the lustrous mink—would be hidden from the camera's eye. Before the camera, the furs carefully arranged on my body, I was warned, "*Ne bougez plus!*" Don't move. Later, in the darkroom, an airbrush would erase a hint of shadow under my eyes, carve an even narrower waist—creating the final touch of perfection. I would find that the camera mysteriously added pounds to the body and emphasized shadowed planes on the face. Its single eye had the power to artfully transform its subject.

Guy, a complete stranger to me until the photo session, was generous with his moral support, frequently reassuring me during the seven hours I spent posing that I was going to be a success. Before I left, he gave me the names of Mme. Dillet at *Vogue* and Eliot Roux at *Elle*, explaining that both women would be interested in booking me for editorial photos. In Paris, as in New York, models were paid very well—and there were no agents to take a percentage of the earnings. In addition, because of the peculiar bureaucratic quagmire that ruled the French workplace, you could not legally earn money unless you had a work permit, but it was virtually impossible to get a work permit. As a result, freelance income was untaxed and effectively hidden, since foreigners were not allowed a bank account. Modeling assignments were divided into prestigious editorial spreads paying $15 an hour; advertising account shoots paid $25 an hour and more and were, then as now, intensely competitive. It was a far cry from the hundreds and even thousands of dollars an hour for editorial spreads that top models earn today. But in 1954, with the favorable dollar to franc rate of exchange, I was earning a very comfortable income. Though I had never worked as a model in New York, I was compensated as if I had.

No amount of experience could take the place of a photo-genic face—the newer, the better. Fashion feeds on novelty and tires quickly of itself. There was no such thing as a learning curve—only the strange trajectory of leaping from nowhere to fifteen minutes of fame and then back to nowhere again.

M. Saad's wife, Denise, was the editor-in-chief of *L'Art et La Mode* and George, her art and photography director. It would be her editorial decision that determined which photos would appear in the magazine. Her mission was to present only French couturier clothes and fabrics, all of French manufacture, a typically chauvinistic editorial policy. George Saad rarely used foreign mannequins. I was lucky enough to be an exception.

By five o'clock in the afternoon, all six furs had finally been photographed. I had been standing in front of the camera for seven hours without a break for so much as a cup of coffee. October in Paris is a particularly beautiful time of year, with warm sunshine and cool, fresh air. The climate control was perfect, but no matter, the photo session had consumed even my prodigious reserves of energy. With only small windows to the outside world, the dark, airless studio was an exhausting venue.

A fourteenth-century poem by Deschamps begins *"Suis je, suis je, suis je belle..."* Am I beautiful? I wondered. I was five feet ten inches tall in my stocking feet and very thin at 115 pounds (my appetite for rich French food never added an ounce of weight). As I wrote the names of editors and other fashion contacts in my notebook, I knew only that my appearance, to my surprise, meant I could stay in Paris. That was enough. *Ca suffit*!

The offices of French *Vogue* were in an ornate *hotel particulier*, surrounded by an impressive wrought-iron fence, on the place du Palais Bourbon. When I arrived there the next day, still uncertain of my new role as professional model, I stood awkwardly in the reception room, where a small woman was sitting at a large, brass-trimmed antique desk. Her black hair pulled back in a stern chignon, she set her dark eyes on me as if she were searching for something. This was Madame Dillet, a power to be reckoned with—she booked all the modeling assignments for *Vogue* and for most of the largest commercial accounts as well. In a city dominated by fashion, she was as close to a modeling agent as existed in the Paris of the 1950s. Her piercing gaze missed nothing, but though she looked fierce, she was actually rather maternal and very kind.

In proper sequence, she introduced me to Edmonde Charles-Roux, the editor-in-chief of French *Vogue*, and Santé Forlano, an American fashion photographer who lived in Paris. Santé brought out his Rolleiflex camera, the famous "Rollie" that the best photographers used, and while I posed near the large bay windows of the reception room, he took a roll of black and white pictures. I looked like a schoolgirl who was skipping class—black turtleneck, gray flannel jumper and short hair with straight bangs. But Santé and his camera saw great possibilities. As we parted—and at these moments I was always numbed by the speed with which decisions about me were made—Santé said, "Remember, I discovered you!"

My next appointment to see Eliot Roux, the American woman who was the fashion editor of *Elle* magazine, was rewarding, but different. Something about her reaction disturbed me. Perhaps because she was also American, she scrutinized me with a sharper eye. I felt that I was not admired (another weapon of the fashion trade—get rid of that model she looks like Godzilla). I was inexperienced and vulnerable enough to be easily intimidated, even a little frightened. Could it be that my successful shoot of the day before was simply an accident, a one-shot event? But, in spite of her hostility, I was booked for fashion editorial photos the following week.

While I was in her office, there was a photo session in progress in the open studio. I watched, dazzled, as Suzy Parker, the first American supermodel, posed for the *Elle* photographer. Her thick, reddish blond hair was loosely curled. She wore a bright red sweater and gray skirt and sat on a bench in front of a sweep of white paper holding a perfume bottle—the real focus of the picture—in her hand. While the photographer adjusted his camera and the lighting, she waited passively, her face bland and expressionless. At his signal, her face suddenly became animated, shining like polished stone under the popping flash camera. As the photographer gave directions, she moved quickly and gracefully into different poses like a wired doll, her radiantly smiling face bathed in the brilliant aura of strobe lights. "*Merveilleuse*," the photographer said, "*Jolie, jolie, tres jolie*." The session continued—Suzy always lapsing into a relaxed, expressionless persona only to turn suddenly vivacious when the photographer was ready to shoot. She was the consummate professional. No extra movement, no emotion wasted. I would eventually learn to perform like that, but in the beginning I tended to squander my emotions on photography shoots. But then, I was a communicator. Suzy didn't seem to mind that no one expected or wanted her to speak, but for me, the rule of silence was hard to observe. Later I was told that she was working in Paris for a year because she owed American taxes. Thanks to the idiosyncratic French system, she paid no taxes because she was not officially employed, so she was able to keep 100 percent of her earnings. The business of French fashion was so vital to the economy that bureaucratic details, like taxing foreigners, were completely overlooked; for once, a French regulation that worked in someone's favor.

In late November, having just finished a photo session at *Elle*, I was hurrying along rue du Faubourg Saint-Honoré, hoping to find a taxi. It was five o'clock and already dark as midnight. Clutching the shawl collar of my black wool coat closed against the biting wind and slices of cold rain, I paused at a kiosk on the corner of Place de la Concorde. I was stunned to see my color photograph on the cover of the prominently displayed *L'Art et La Mode*. The title alone, "Art and Fashion," conveyed the spirit of Paris fashion in the fifties. I had not heard from George Saad since that October day when he had photographed me in Revillon furs. There had been no mention of the fate of the pictures. I was amazed to see myself, wrapped in sumptuous mink, a hint of a smile on my face.

"*C'est moi!*" I exclaimed enthusiastically to the laconic *propriétaire*, pointing to the prominently displayed copy of *L'Art et La Mode*. He looked at the magazine, then at me. Smiling cynically, he explained condescendingly that the cover was a picture of a famous model. "*Ca n'est pas vous, mademoiselle. C'est un mannequin qui est bien connue.*" Not you, but a famous fashion model. I grabbed a copy of the magazine and held it beside my face. "*Oui, c'est moi.*" I insisted. He shook his head. "*Ça n'est pas vous.*" He refused to believe that the American girl standing before him in the icy downpour was the glamorous, mink-clad figure on the magazine cover. So I learned what it meant to be photogenic. The eye of the camera is the eye of the beholder, the arbiter of beauty. In the strange grammar of fashion, I had become, at that moment, both subject and object. I felt profoundly displaced seeing the perfected version of my face gazing at me from the cover of a magazine.

I was never again quite so impressed by the transforming power of a photograph, all the more magical because I had not anticipated it. I had the sensation of being in two places at once—alive, shivering on a Paris street, and immobile in print. That projection of reality would become part of my disguise, and I wore it proudly. I was not perfect, but my photographs were.

I have rarely been happier than I was that night as I stood in the cold rain contemplating not the future, but the reality of the present. I paid the proprietor of the kiosk for the magazine just as an empty taxi finally appeared, and I was driven to the Hotel de Nice clutching the copy of *L'Art et la Mode* to my modest bosom.

Ironically, I never posed for Saad again. Four editorial pages of the magazine were devoted to black and white photos of me, wearing the other furs that I had modeled, but future issues of *L'Art et La Mode* appeared without me.

The dramatic change in my circumstances was hard to absorb. I felt as if I was living a dream, a fantasy story of the small town Ohio girl who becomes a Paris model. I was finally the most important person in my own life, and as a new model I would become important to the Paris fashion world. Dinner dates with earnest escorts, young Americans and Frenchmen, often followed by performances of plays and operas, would become almost nightly events. My life was leaping ahead, a little like a car that had gone out of gear. I had never been the focus of such attention and it changed the nature of my introspections. The rush of euphoria from this new drug made me an instant addict.

Several days after my magazine cover photo first appeared, to my amazement, I received a call from the *Paris Herald Tribune*. An excited young woman, Mr. Brunswick's assistant, informed me that there was finally an opening for me at the paper. I was too stunned to frame a coherent reply until she continued with the job description—I would man the Teletype with the world's news rolling in, from midnight until six in the morning. It was "a foot in the door" and not without future journalistic opportunities. But, I didn't hesitate to say "No, thank you," and hastily explained that my photo had recently appeared on the cover of *L'Art et la Mode*, launching my new career as a fashion model. "But don't you want to work for the *Tribune?*" her voice was insistent. She didn't want to end the conversation without hiring me, and I was appalled, both at the harsh nature of the work, even for a young woman, and at the small weekly sum they were offering to pay, significantly less than I earned in a day of modeling. In retrospect, as I struggled to become a writer years later, I often felt I might have prospered after all if I'd said "Yes" to that offer. But I stuck to my decision to continue down the path that had opened before me, though I still look back with nostalgia to the road not taken.

The friends who had been with me as we walked the quais of the Seine that Sunday afternoon when my future was still being decided were not as fortunate as I was. Less than two years later, Fred died of hepatitis in Greece without finishing a single novel. Before his premature death from a heart attack, Christopher had established his reputation as a Left Bank poet. But by then, he had left a second wife, Juditte, and two young sons. He died in Majorca at age thirty-five. Marjorie remained in Paris, but she was never a close friend and we lost touch. I knew as little about her background as she did about mine. But we knew each other well enough to know there was no common ground.

l'art et la
mode
DE PARIS

# 6

# *Always In Vogue*

adame Biguet's kindness notwithstanding, after more
than three months in Paris, it was time to leave the
Hotel de Nice. Holly and Jack had found an apartment, and the Staffords had moved into a suite of rooms with
a tiny kitchen in the building next to the hotel. I was spending
most of each day tearing around Paris by taxi, going from one
photograph shoot to another, from *Vogue* to *Marie Claire* to *Elle*
and back to *Vogue*. Madame Biguet was not happy about the
numerous phone calls I received every day from photographers
and editors, which kept the small hotel desk frantically busy.
She was anxious to return to the calm that had reigned before
I took over the phone lines, dysfunctional as they were.

As my life got more complicated, the charm of my tiny
garret had begun to pale. Without an agent, I was forced
to be my own secretary as well as my own accountant. My
small address book bulged with extra scraps of paper—phone
numbers, appointment dates and addresses. Every time I had
a phone call at the Hotel de Nice, I had to rush down the
six flights of narrow stairs to the lobby, or endure the painfully slow birdcage elevator's descent. The longer I stayed in

Saint-Germain, the more restaurants I discovered and I was limiting my gastronomic vocabulary by eating at the Hotel de Nice every night.

I had arrived in Paris with two pairs of shoes—brown penny loafers and black flats. Models were expected to bring all their own makeup and a pair of black high heeled pumps to every photography session. I went to a custom shoe store on Avenue Mantignon where I paid an exorbitant price for a pair of black leather high heels, even as the clerk shook her head over my size 10 feet. The best match was still much too small.

Wearing the painfully tight shoes (I had just ended a long day of modeling raincoats for *Vogue*), I attended my first French party in mid-November. My hostess, Jacqueline Sirot, was a vivacious, very pretty young Parisian who had met a college classmate of mine, Jeanne Siegfried, when both were summer interns at Lord & Taylor in New York. The Sirot apartment on rue Saint-Honoré had no rugs or curtains and was sparsely furnished. Since their main residence was an elegant townhouse on the place du Trocadero, the modest apartment was purposely left unadorned to avoid French taxes, which were levied for the value of furnishings and creature comforts rather than for the value of the real estate itself.

It was a complex family, with half-siblings and stepparents and a mixture of Jewish and Catholic faiths. All the children, enough to make a large party in themselves, seemed to be in attendance that night. I was exhausted from posing in a chill mist on the banks of the Seine, and my feet ached from their tight confinement. I slumped on the couch, shoes off, too tired to be decorous. The voluble young Sirots and their other guests sat on the floor, discussing the latest films in rapid French.

Intricate analysis of French and foreign films was a favorite pastime for them, but my language skills were still limited and in any case, I was too tired to concentrate, so I retreated into a baffled silence. Interrupting my distracted state, a young blond woman sat down beside me, introducing herself as Barbara Sutton. We quickly discovered that we were both newcomers to Paris. Barbara was working as a journalist for *U.S. News and World Report*. She had met the Sirot family during her junior year abroad when she lived in their formal family residence on the place du Trocadero. Before she was offered a job as a journalist in Paris, she had been working as a researcher for *Time* in New York, but had already planned to leave that post. In 1954, *Time* did not allow women to rise above the rank of researcher and Barbara was determined to be a writer. We continued talking until the party ended, exchanging phone numbers as we parted. Our friendship, held together by our mutual fascination with Paris and everything French, continued for decades. When I left Paris two years later, Barbara stayed and eventually married a charming young Hungarian engineer, Laurent Wollak, who provided her with everything her generous parents had not: a lovely apartment in Saint-Cloud, a summer house in Chantilly. She and Laurent had two handsome sons and a beautiful daughter.

After the party at their home, Jacqueline Sirot's intense but charming brother, Paul, became one of my escorts. We had some especially good evenings at a small *boite* called Whiskey A Go-go, a popular night spot where the novel (for the French) entertainment was dancing to big band tunes played on a 1940s American jukebox, drinking *"le whisky"* and talking about the virtues of *"le Buick."* Paul often invited me to his father's elegant apartment, where a servant prepared and served the formal dinners. M. Sirot was lively and urbane, and from his spot at the head of the table would quiz me about the details of my work as a model. He seemed amused by my stories of the eccentricities of the fashion world, where arrogance was often laced with cruelty. If the editors were not rude to me, they were berating the photographer and elbowing each other.

Because Paul was shy and quiet in his father's presence, I too was often ill at ease. But I was fascinated with the portrait of bourgeois French life that unfolded. When the Sirots divorced, Madame Sirot had remarried a man who was Catholic, and the family enlarged to include the children of three marriages. Since I was accustomed to the simpler households of my Midwest, I was intrigued by the diversity. The Sirots were endlessly entertaining and full of enthusiasm for the life in their native Paris.

When Barbara and I discovered that we were both looking for more spacious living arrangements, we decided to combine our search. Apartments in an overcrowded postwar Paris were prohibitively expensive, if you were lucky enough to find one. The reality of the situation was brought home to me when, one day at *Vogue*, I overheard Madame Dillet discussing an apartment in an elegant Right Bank home that had recently become available. She hesitated before giving me the address and phone number, perhaps because she suspected that the result would be disappointiing. Rather than waste precious time, I phoned from the reception room at *Vogue*. In my now well-accented French, I explained to the person who answered the phone that I had heard about the apartment. "*Oui, il y a un apartment.*" May I see it? "*Quel est votre nom, mademoiselle?*"

she asked me, rather imperiously. *"Je m'appele Mademoiselle Ann Montgomery et je travaille comme mannequin chez le journal* Vogue." There was a long, meaningful silence and then she said, *"Votre nom est de Montgomery?"* *"Pas le 'de', Madame,"* I answered honestly (in France, a "de" before the last name implies an aristocratic, titled name). *"Simplement Montgomery."* To my great amusement, she said abruptly, *"Pas d'apartement,"* and immediately hung up the phone.

After that experience, Barbara and I focused our search on hotels in Saint-Germain-des-Prés. In postwar Paris, even the likes of Simone de Beauvoir lived in a hotel room. We chose the Hotel Welcome, a modest, almost shabby, cream-colored stucco building on the corner of boulevard Saint-Germain and rue de Seine, not far from the Hotel de Nice. Rue de Seine, the market street, allowed only pedestrian traffic and had a jovial, village ambiance that I found comforting. The hotel's double glass and wrought-iron entrance was next to the horse-meat butcher shop, a uniquely French purveyor, announced by a handsome gilt horse's head above its red storefront. I never knew how the Hotel Welcome got its English name, but it was distinguished by large rooms with floor-to-ceiling windows that opened onto boulevard Saint-Germain, filling the room with light. Each room had a washbasin and a bidet, very continental, both with lots of hot running water—definitely not continental. In the French style to which I was becoming accustomed, each floor had a toilet off the hallway. The radiators actually provided enough warmth for the bitter cold Paris winter that was to follow. A tough Parisienne, Madame Guillies, and her somewhat gentler sister, both bleached blondes, were the managers, enforcing their rules in a tyrannical manner.

Since most of the hotel residents were transients, the sisters were probably amazed to see two American girls who actually wanted to rent by the month. The main rule: No men were allowed to spend the night without paying. We thought this was hilariously funny since we would never have allowed our dates to come to our rooms. But the tough-minded blonds were taking no chances.

In mid-December, Barbara rented a room on the third floor and I, Number 10, a room on the second. After the confines of my garret, it was liberating to be able to open the tall French windows to the tiny balustrade that overlooked the lively tempo of Left Bank life on boulevard Saint-Germain. I purchased a small alcohol burner that boiled water in minutes and a French coffee pot to make my own morning coffee. With my one small saucepan I could even boil an egg. My room was simply furnished with a table that served as a desk and a comfortable double bed where I could easily sprawl in a diagonal snow-angel posture, submerged in the comfort of deep sleep. The only other furniture was a large armoire, with double doors that never closed properly, a serious inconvenience since it served as my bank as well as a closet. As my fashion shoots increased, my income—always received in cash—increased as well. French money looked gigantic compared to the few trim American dollars I still had in an envelope. With its colorful portraits of saints and political leaders drawn against historic French buildings, it seemed more like Monopoly money than legal tender. These enormous pieces of paper continued to pile up in the bottom of my armoire. When I needed cash, I simply reached in the bottom and pulled some out. Whatever came up always seemed to be enough. I was earning a substantial income, more than adequate for my needs, and I never really kept a precise tally. The maid who cleaned my room every day never touched the contents of the armoire, so far as I know. But if she had taken a few of my hard-earned francs, I might not have missed them. A bit cavalier, of course, but between long hours of work and the daily frustrations of Parisian life—endless waits in cold winter rain to trap one of the taxis speeding past, then traveling through crowded streets with chaotic traffic patterns—I had other things on my mind. One day a week was given over to the complexities of collecting my earnings. It often took several visits to collect the money I was owed from various photographers and magazine business managers. One of my defense mechanisms was to downplay the importance of money, my own version of *noblesse oblige*.

Barbara's independent lifestyle had become well established, aided by, I suspected, a small trust fund as well as her salary. In the fifties, she could afford to indulge her taste for exotic foreign ports and, it turned out, a passion for a foreign correspondent in Viet Nam. Dwight Martin was tall, blond and ruggedly handsome. He was the quintessential trenchcoat journalist, inviting risk, taking one difficult assignment after another for *Time* magazine. While covering the war in Vietnam, during the most intense years of battle between the French and the Viet Cong, he contracted a fatal case of amoebic dysentery. But long before his untimely death, Barbara spent the spring of 1955 organizing visas and travel to Vietnam for a tryst. I would pass her as she rushed down the stairs of the Hotel Welcome. She was in a mildly manic state, clutching foreign visas and travel permits, saying, "I haven't got a minute...I'm going to Saigon," (a place I had never heard of). And by July 15, she was gone, filing stories with *U.S. News and World Report* to cover the trip. We, the Americans in Paris, saw the war as none of our affair. It was waged by the French, desperately trying to keep their colonial control of Vietnam from falling into the hands of the Viet Cong. We didn't know that our country, through clandestine military and intelligence support, was already involved in that war. In Paris, we saw the banners flapping in the wind above the place de la Concorde. *"Sauvez Dienbienfu!"* We had no idea it meant us. When accused of sending "military advisors" to Vietnam by the French cognoscente we met in Left Bank cafés, we vigorously denied any complicity. It's your colonial war, we assured the French. America doesn't play that game.

I continued to eat in restaurants for lunch and for dinner every evening, usually at the *Vagenende*, a simple Alsatian bistro on boulevard Saint-Germain, just a block and a half from my hotel that served delicious food. *Cotelettes, fois de veau* and *fillet mignon garni avec pommes frites*, all served with pungent wine sauces, led the menu. Between the main meal and desert, a fresh green salad was served with a platter of a several cheeses, from which the diner would make a selection. The waiters knew how to mix a superior salad dressing at the table using only a large spoon and a fork—a pouring, mixing and balancing act that I always watched with fascination. The meal ended with a cup of espresso coffee to neutralize the effects of the half carafe of *vin ordinaire* I could never resist.

News of the comfort and unbelievably low rent at the Hotel Welcome had spread. A few weeks after we moved in, Susan Brady, another friend, dissatisfied with the rustic accommodations of *la Cité* (residential housing for foreign students attending the Sorbonne), took the room on the top floor. Susan, already fluent in French, was a talented writer whose name had been given to me by my former boyfriend, a lawyer in New York. From Hunter College she had come to Paris on a Fulbright Scholarship and like the rest of us, thought her life changed forever. I found her very intelligent and amusing. Though our families were not really alike, each was dysfunctional in its own way. Susan's family was afflicted with the Irish disease, alcoholism, and its effect on families was not unlike that of the mental disease that plagued my own family. If she experienced constraints growing up with her parents and three brothers in a small Bronx apartment, they were rarely mentioned. Education and the adventure of foreign travel took precedence over everything. She was, as her French boyfriend Philippe often said, *"très sympathique."* I personally found most French men diffident and lacking energy, but Susan adored Philippe, a young medical student laboriously studying to become a doctor. In France, medical school admissions were based not only on ability but also on a quota system. The object of the quota was to keep the number of graduates at a certain level. Otherwise, in a small country like France, it would be difficult to find a place to practice medicine. He was a conscientious student who worked hard to keep his privileged position. On more than one occasion after I had worked long hours for several days in a row, Susan and Philippe would rescue me by taking me out to dinner.

Barbara, Susan and I, like three college roommates, often shared late-night discussions. Our three perspectives on Paris life, that of the journalist, the student and the fashion model created wonderful conversations. Barbara, ever the professional journalist, was a clever interpreter of expatriate life. Her worldly knowledge was the result of having grown up in Buenos Aires, where her father was a corporate executive for an American company. At age sixteen, she had returned to the United States to attend Wellesley College. It was Susan's theory that because the French took refuge behind *la vie privée,* the hedge for their cultural reserve and distrust of foreigners, we Americans were free not only of the conventions of life in the United States, but of the French as well. *Vie privée*, literally "private life," the barrier that even long association and friendship could never completely penetrate, meant we existed outside society's acceptance or rejection. I thought this was a novel idea. The intensity of our involvement with expatriate life was easily tolerated. We were young and energetic and loved every minute of it.

The novelty of my new life had created an intense need for a sympathetic ear. I was managing all my own appointments, following up work with trips to photographers and magazines to collect payment and there were many times when the pace of the fashion world left me breathless. At other times, I found it hideously boring. As an admired and successful fashion model, I should have been confident, at least, of my appearance. Instead, I had serious doubts about my looks and was plagued by my imperfections, real and imagined. Like most American girls and women, I was indoctrinated by fashion magazines to admire perfection in feminine beauty. As it turned out, it was pure luck that my DNA had blessed me with the tall thin body that had become fashion's icon. But in the Midwest, my kind of beauty, if it was that, had never been admired.

# Chapter 6

The tedium of modeling was a result of the "hurry-up-and-wait" ethic of the fashion world that applied mostly to the hapless model. The preparations created hours of inactivity, empty time spent waiting for editors and photographers to assemble and finally begin the photo shoot. In Paris, to further complicate the scene, no one was ever on time. Once the photographer and the editor did arrive, more time was spent choosing a site for the photos, selecting the clothes that the model or models would wear. The models stood for long hours, with poses directed by the photographer, by now the central player, as he endlessly adjusted the lighting and the aperture of his camera.

On one occasion, I arrived promptly at 3 p.m. for a photo shoot at an elegant Right Bank address. A sweet but noncommittal French maid opened the door for me and showed me into the drawing room, where I sat for four hours. I was not prepared for this long wait and soon tired of daydreaming, creating interior dialogue of what it would be like to live in such splendor—gilt-framed mirrors, Aubusson carpets, exquisite Louis Quatorze furniture. Finally, an aristocratic woman, the owner, appeared, looking ragged and fatigued. I launched into a rare tirade, expressing my outrage at the long wait. "Well, " she retorted, "what do you care? You're being paid by the hour." Her editorial job with *Marie Claire* had kept her too long at the office and, as it turned out, the shoot had been summarily canceled. She finally managed a brief apology, and I was unceremoniously ushered out the door, still angry. Ordinarily I wouldn't have risked such a reaction, but the degree of success I had gained was changing me. Besides, I always took great care to be punctual.

Several days later I went to the *blanchisserie* that always washed and ironed my small supply of underwear and cotton blouses. It was past six and I had posed all day for two different photographers. I waited impatiently as the proprietor slowly searched for my package, found it and pulled it off the shelf. When he examined my ticket, he replaced the bundle of clean laundry without handing it to me. *"Je suis desole, mademoiselle"* he explained, *"mais le ticket est pour demain soir, pas pour aujourd'hui."* The laundry ticket said delivery would be tomorrow, not tonight. I stared at him in disbelief. Raising my voice, I said that I worked as hard as he did in this life and that I wouldn't tolerate his behavior. He replied by shaking his head and repeating that I could pick up the laundry *"demain."* I stared at the short, dark-haired man and shouted—in his language of course, not mine: "Give me my laundry!" With a terrified expression on his face, while his wife watched in horror, he retreated to the shelves and returned with my package. I paid and left without the usual *"Merci, monsieur."* I had won out, for once, against Gallic contrariness.

It was difficult to disabuse the outside world of the notion that a career as a fashion photographer's model was not all glamour. I often felt I deserved sympathy for my hard work. Today, one would say that I was crying all the way to the bank. My American friends listened, however skeptically, to my complaints about rude photographers, haughty fashion editors and impatient clients. Barbara, understandably tired of hearing my complaints, finally said, "But Ann, the woods are full of pretty girls." Her comment reminded me that posing for a photographer was more than simply holding still while someone snapped the shutter. If the woods are full of pretty girls, then all the pretty girls could be models, or better yet, actresses. Obviously, other ingredients went into the mix—an ability to project an image, an awareness of how to move your body. But even this realization did not insulate me from negative feelings. There were days when I actively hated clothes, and often the heavy makeup for photos made my face break out in blotches. On my own time, I wore the same turtleneck sweaters and plaid pleated skirts I had worn in college. It made me feel safe from the commercialization of myself that I justifiably feared. I was always upset when someone would say, "Oh, wasn't it exciting to wear all those beautiful clothes!" No, clothes may enhance a woman's attributes, but only a Barbie would imagine that clothes could change a woman or substitute for solid accomplishment in some arena of life. Another distressing question: "Did they give you the clothes you wore?" Lend, yes; give, never. Why would anyone assume that a working fashion model would be indulged like a debutante? And then, thoroughly disappointed with my replies, "But, you could buy the clothes that were made for you, couldn't you?" Yes, one could buy a Chanel suit for about two thousand American dollars, at the 1950s rate of exchange. One could, I could not. One of my favorite games as a child had been playing dress-up. Fanciful clothes created from my mother's few cast-offs were the props of my child's world of make believe, but my childhood was past. I was in Paris, reveling in my freedom. I sensed that it might be short-lived, and rich clothing would only slow me down. My most frequent complaint was that I had become an object—a human clothes hanger for expensive couture apparel.

Shortly after I began modeling for *Vogue*, I was asked to go on French television. At the broadcast station, I was politely introduced to the panel of an intellectual talk show and given an exquisite, vividly spangled bolero of many colors to wear. Richly embroidered with sequins, reminiscent of a toreador's jacket, it was created by Elsa Schiaparelli, the famous designer and star of the panel. That jacket's fame resurfaced when, years later, it was featured at an exhibit of Schiaparelli's designs at the Costume Institute of the Metropolitan Museum of Art. During the television talk show, she discussed her approach to fashion, her preference for elegance and the look of opulence. A tall, imperious Italian woman, she cherished her high rank in Paris couture and had an aura of class that set her a bit apart from the competition. In France, fashion was respected and treated as a serious subject for the intelligentsia, at least as important to the national economy as any work of literature. The august panel dismissed me once the elegant jacket had been shown to the television audience. I remember thinking, but I'm intelligent and I have opinions about fashion. Why not talk to me? Because, my dear, they would have explained, you are just a mannequin, a term we use in America for the fashion dummies in department store windows.

In my free hours, I saw the tourist's Paris—every statue, every stone-carved cathedral—and stared in awe at the stained-glass windows that suffused my face with bright dots of color in the dimly lit interiors. The Orangerie, a small museum in the Jardin des Tuileries, was my favorite. Monet's giant and extravagantly beautiful water lilies were the only paintings on its circular walls. The water lilies seemed to float in air, unattached to anything as mundane as canvas. My many trips to the *Louvre*—so dark and imposing—lacked the intimacy and pure pleasure of the *Orangerie*. Accompanied by friends,

I never missed a single new exposition and frequently took day trips, sightseeing in the beautiful French countryside.

As serious gourmets, we were constantly researching and grading the inexpensive restaurants that we chose when an escort wasn't paying the check. I preferred dinner dates with one of the many American graduate students, earnest young men whose impressive ambitions usually far exceeded my own.

While I was living in New York City, when I was supposed to be finishing my sophomore year of college, I had met a tall, handsome blond Norwegian, Per Arneberg. For some reason I cannot recall how we met but it became a special relationship. His father was Oslo's premier architect and had been chosen to design one of the conference rooms in the United Nations Building in New York. Per proudly gave me a tour of the elegant chamber; its walls were covered in silky blue fabric sprinkled with silver stars and it was furnished with ranks of blue upholstered theater seats. On the sweeping dais was a large polished wood conference table, lending a proper note of solemnity. I was suitably impressed.

After our trip to the U.N., we went to Greenwich Village for dinner, engrossed in each other as we talked about the many contrasting worlds of New York—the bohemian flair of Greenwich Village, the sober, granite barrens of the financial district and the elegance of the Upper East Side townhouses. In spite of his quiet Nordic cool, Per was gentle and even amorous, and I was definitely attracted to him. Shortly after we met, my mother's illness forced me to leave New York, but, to my surprise, he loyally kept in touch. He sent me a dozen red roses for my twentieth birthday in June; they provided a uniquely formal decoration on the dining room table of my home on

Church Street. In Ohio's oppressive July heat and humidity he flew from New York for a weekend visit. I was uneasy during his stay, unable to recapture the intimacy of our urban romance in Oxford's stifling summer weather. The proximity of my childhood world effectively killed the romance. At one point my father insisted we take my sister, then a talkative eleven-year-old, on our walk through the college campus. I tried to refuse this invasion of privacy but, as always, my father won out. Stripped of its mystery, my fledgling relationship floundered. Fortunately, Per seemed oblivious to my discomfort and anxiety. He charmed my father (my mother was hospitalized at the time) and managed to be calmly reassuring to me. We corresponded a few times after that but he eventually returned to Norway and disappeared, permanently, I thought, into his own family and culture.

Then, quite unexpectedly, after I had been in Paris for almost two months, Per reappeared in my life. He had called my father to get my address since, his education finished in Norway, he was returning to New York to take a job with a Norwegian shipping company. Then twenty-three, he arrived at my hotel, poised and properly suited. He had reserved a table at the Tour D'Argent, at that time the most elegant restaurant in Paris. The large windows of the fifth-floor dining room overlooked the Seine and Paris, spread out on either bank like a sequined shawl. The pale blue November sky, still light at eight o'clock, and myriad candles gave the room a soft glow. The food was certainly excellent. Unfortunately, accustomed to smaller portions at modest Left Bank bistros, I was unable to finish the enormous lamb chop that followed a dozen perfect oysters. Even though we drank a lot of champagne, my appetite did not revive. The more ardent Per's overtures, the more I retreated into myself, nervously hedging his questions. Since I had been in Paris such a short time, I was still anxious about the future. At that point I had not begun my career as a fashion model and I was afraid that I might have to return to America. This time my uncertainty was catching and when we kissed good-bye at my hotel, it was for the last time. Thirty years later, I saw a picture in *Town & Country* magazine of Per, with his American wife and three children, skiing in Davos, Switzerland. Again, I was suitably impressed.

Recalling these ardent young men makes them seem like prizefighters that somehow entered my life. I was the prize—or might have been if beauty's promise could ever be fulfilled. These admirers plunged into my ring; then down and out to the count after leaning exhausted on the ropes, they retreated. They would disappear, as if to say, no more of this pointless game. Then a replacement would appear, fresh and feisty, ready to wage the battle for my affections. My bouts of self-loathing, handmaiden to my depressions, increased the chances of evenhanded rejection of all players, though the final punch could come from either side.

When Sam Paschal appeared in my life, solid and protective, he seemed the perfect antidote to the bitter continental winter. Sam had a swimmer's physique—his muscular shoulders slightly bent forward as if reaching for the next wave. His handsome face was always creased with a self-effacing smile. We were almost the same height and when he put his arm around me, I felt as if we were a perfect fit. He was very concerned about my precarious financial situation and twice set up a small savings account in my name at his New York bank, which I,

twice, returned to him. I was grateful for his support, but I
didn't want anyone's money but my own. Besides, though I had
a bad habit of complaining about financial insecurities, I was
beginning to make more than enough money as a model to
fund my modest lifestyle. There was no question that he wanted
to rescue me. When the weather was warmer, he insisted that
I take up my tennis game again; he played the other side of
the court to encourage me. He had a small coterie of friends
from his rich New York life who were also studying in Paris.
Whenever we encountered them at Left Bank restaurants the
young women in the group would glare at me and turn away.
I did not fail to get the message, but wondered why they were
so disturbed. I guess they thought Sam belonged to their social
milieu, not mine.

He once wrote to me, enclosing ninety dollars in traveler's
checks, with some surprisingly prescient cautions: "I am
confident that you will always be active in those ways which
particularly appeal to people who don't have direction—who
can't enjoy close-angle navigating." Of my Left Bank crowd
he said, "Your friends seem to lack conviction. If they seem
totally out of control, coach them. They may be up against
overwhelming impulses and complications." I was very attracted
to his well-meaning attempts to direct my life and would have
happily forged a stronger bond between us. When I refused to
accept the money, he was quite upset. This was as close as he
wanted to be. It seemed to him to mean that I was refusing to
accept him as a friend, even though I thought him the most
admirable of the young men I knew. The last time I saw him,
he was about to return to the States to summer on Long Island
with his family and then finish his senior year at Amherst. Years

## Chapter 6

later when he married, there was a large wedding picture on the Society page of the *New York Times*, showing Sam with his bride leaving Riverside Cathedral. Only then did I realize how wealthy he was.

Sandy-haired Bob Ketchum, a tall, rangy American student at the Sorbonne, was the most attentive of my dinner dates. He and my friends Linley and Barbara Stafford had forged a tight circle around me. They thought he was the perfect foil for my bohemian lifestyle. Bob was certainly serious about his life and would have provided a very solid base for any woman he married. He was muscular, slender and taller than I was, but I couldn't quite give him the passionate affection he craved. He couldn't give me the reassurance of the strength of his attraction without that. When competing desires collide in the space between two people, the feelings self-destruct. The Staffords always felt Bob would have been my perfect mate. The man I chose instead was someone Bob claimed "would destroy me," if I didn't destroy him first. "You cannot mix two such strong personalities without courting disaster," he warned. I felt that he was fighting for his relationship with me and dismissed his diatribe as nothing but sour grapes. He invited me to go skiing in Switzerland in March, and initially I agreed. But by the time he pushed the round trip air tickets under my hotel door, I had changed my mind about him and Switzerland. "But you promised!" he complained. My promises weren't worth much in those days.

Bob kept a journal while he was at the Sorbonne, and the following year he wrote to me from the Wharton School, where he was getting a degree in business administration. Reminiscing about his days in Paris and quoting from his journal, he wrote,

"Betty Jeffries introduced me to a college friend from Oxford, Ohio—one Miss Ann Montgomery....Found her to be working as a model here in Paris—in lieu of continuing her studies—she majored in French. Went to Le Select where we talked...Ann tainted with the fast-fading stain of a 'College Girl Personality,' but this irritating aspect completely eclipsed by the qualities of intellect so lavishly displayed in our discussion. Thoroughly enjoyed this contact." From the Wharton School, Bob went on to Harvard and a life somewhere else, leaving me this flattering portrait of my young self in Paris.

I had been in love only once before, with a graduate student from Northwestern University I met at a New Year's Eve party during my freshman year at college. He drove me home from the party; I was hopelessly drunk and hopelessly infatuated. His dark good looks—luminous brown eyes, curly brown hair—and his intelligence made him irresistible. He returned to the Northwestern campus right after we met and I wrote him an impassioned poem about our encounter. He was charmed, but I was only eighteen and far better at handling an epistolary relationship than the intimacy of physical togetherness. He took me to a formal dance during his spring vacation and as the evening ended, he said adoringly, "I think I have to marry you." I pulled away from him in despair. Marriage? Impossible. I was much too young for marriage. I had already planned a summer in Colorado, my first prolonged stay away from home, and no mere romance could make me change those plans. So I turned him down, then he turned me down, and then I was grievously wounded. It was true love after all. Until I felt that way again, I would not get seriously involved with any other man.

# Chapter 6

During my first winter in Paris, I was flattered to be pursued by André, a young French count. André was a handsome blond man in his early thirties who was painfully overburdened by his family's expectations for him. He liked to drink champagne and go dancing at the Elephant Blanc, a popular Left Bank nightclub. Otherwise, he seemed to have few ambitions. I found his reserve charming, though the nightlife he enjoyed seemed bland and uninteresting to me. I liked to go out with him because he was attentive without being aggressive and never pressed me into a closer relationship. But he kept calling and taking me to one expensive restaurant or *boîte de nuit* after another. We had been dating for a couple of months when he invited me to meet his family. On a lovely spring Sunday, we drove his small sports convertible, with the top down, through the Normandy countryside. The family country house was a ponderous, turreted stone manse. His mother, who greeted us at the huge wooden door, was barely hospitable. What I saw reflected in her gaze when she looked at me was all too familiar. I was beautiful yes, but not for her son. She made some mysterious signal to André and he explained that no, of course, we were not planning to stay for lunch. Then she formally dismissed herself and disappeared into her gloomy castle. To escape, I pretended to have an urgent appointment back in Paris. I was relieved when the young Count stopped calling; I was much happier with the casual social life of Left Bank cafés and the company of other young American students. He was the first and last of my Gallic admirers.

Early in my modeling career, I posed frequently for Guy Arsac, whose assistant, Gislaine, was also his wife and a former model. Arsac was a favorite with the giants of couture—Jacques

Fath, Balmain and Dior—and had huge catalogue-style spreads in *Vogue* of their collections. He could not adjust a light or peer into his camera without saying *"Merde, merde"* thus teaching me my first French curse. Initially, I thought the word was a flattering superlative. It was weeks before I found out the real meaning. His patient wife would stand in the shadows of the strobe lights, silently watching me pose from the fringes of the room. I could not believe it when she told me she too was American. One of my best pictures came from those frosty sessions in his barn like studio. He proudly gave me an enlargement of a fashion photo—me as an incredibly coy Audrey Hepburn look-alike.

In early December, I had my first opportunity to pose for Henry Clarke. He was the top photographer at French *Vogue*. The results of that first photography session were dismal and we disliked each other from the moment we met. I detested his fey arrogance and he treated me as if I were a particularly awkward model. For the photo session, I had worn an unflattering silk print dress with voluminous folds of fabric that nearly buried me. The shot was in color and my hair looked like it had been frizzed and painted with henna. I knew he wasn't pleased with me, but I was trapped into completing the photo session in spite of his hostility.

I was more than ready to leave the studio when we finished the shoot, but Madame Dillet stopped me at the door and begged me to take on one more assignment. Reluctantly, I agreed. She explained that the famous New York photographer Virginia Thoren was in Paris for a short stay and that I should be flattered she was willing to work with me. It was already dark so I took a taxi and, typically, the driver had

trouble finding the obscure Right Bank address. This further exacerbated my black mood.

I entered the dimly lit apartment to be greeted indifferently by a Frenchman holding a camera. He seemed to know that Madame Dillet had booked the shoot and, handing me the Revillon fur I was to wear for the photo, a particularly sumptuous Emba mink, he said, "I am Georges," in heavily accented English. The apartment was so small that the makeshift studio—a large roll of slick white paper and some dark fabric curtains serving as a backdrop for the spotlights—took up most of the living space. Virginia Thoren was nowhere in sight. Instead, this rude Frenchman kept ordering me to modify every pose I tried. "Head up—no to the side. No, no, no. I don't like the way you look." "You look horrible, *terriblement fatiguée.*" After a long afternoon dealing with Henry Clarke's arrogance, I was in no mood for this obnoxious man. I did wonder what had happened to Miss Thoren, the famous fashion photographer, but under orders and strobe lights I found it difficult to think clearly. By then I was not only tired but hungry and more than ready to retreat to the relative comfort of my Left Bank hotel.

*"Je n'aime pas son visage!"* The photographer was raising his voice, talking to an invisible audience, circling me with his demon camera and shouting his disapproval of my appearance. At that moment, the fatigue overwhelmed me and I suddenly started sobbing. Mascara made black trails down my cheeks. I was drowning in my tears, completely unable to stop crying.

Suddenly, a diminutive blond woman came out from behind the dark curtains that surrounded the studio and the dreadful Georges was instantly silenced. I stared in disbelief at this composed, attractive woman who said in perfect English, "Let her pose as she wants." Looking like a whipped dog, he lowered his camera. She gently led me to the bathroom and helped me repair my makeup. "I am Virginia Thoren," she said quietly.

For the rest of the session, she stood within view of both Georges and me. I posed for the camera as I wanted, chin resting on hand. My expression, if anything, was one of relief—or was it insouciance? I was calm again after my stormy tears and my eyes were unusually clear. I never felt better prepared for the camera's eye.

Who was Georges? Virginia Thoren's name appeared on the ad when it was published and she never explained his presence. Was he her lover (she deserves only pity if that were the case), and was she trying to help him establish himself as a fashion photographer? She never explained, and since she worked primarily in New York City, I never had a chance to ask her. I certainly never wanted to tell the story to Madame Dillet or any of the editors, the smart and often disdainful editors, at *Vogue.* I don't know if I even told my friends, because I hated to admit that a Frenchman had broken through my armor of sullen detachment.

It is still my favorite photograph—without compare, the best photograph I ever had taken. As a shell of my usual self, completely drained of emotion, I had become a "natural." In 1955, that advertisement for Revillon furs appeared in so many issues of *Vogue*—French, English and American—that I would have turned a nice profit if they had paid residuals.

Just before I left for my Christmas ski trip in Kitzbühel, Francine du Plessix Gray, a young editor of *Réalités*, called me for a fashion shoot. *Réalités*, published in London, was an elite,

slick magazine of criticism and the arts. It was Francine's enviable job to cover the Paris fashion scene. I later discovered that she had a few important credentials: She was a gifted writer, but also the stepdaughter of Alexander Lieberman, the famed artistic director of American *Vogue*.

Francine booked the *Vogue* photographer Santé Forlano, who had once taken test photos of me. This was to be the first of many times he and I would work together professionally. Francine had explained that she was going to use Charles Addams (creator of the famed, ghoulish Addams family) and his outrageous, uproarious *New Yorker* cartoons as the theme for a fashion feature showing black evening gowns by French couturiers. It was a novel idea but one with little appeal for me, particularly once I saw the props—a human skull, a fresh pig's head (in some quarters of France still considered a delicacy)—and my date, a well known French actor who was a midget, less than four feet tall. I could see the humorous possibilities of our crazy picnic, but as a novice model I didn't want to be an object of derision. When I complained, Francine was nearly hysterical over the possibility that her brilliant idea might fall apart— skulls, pig's head and now the tall skinny model refusing to be photographed. "Oh, please," she said. "It will be such fun!" Even Santé chimed in with "Don't be so serious!"

Of course, Francine prevailed. My eyebrows were partially shaved off and redrawn in thick black lines that swept away from my eyes. Dark blue eye shadow was brushed below my cheeks to create the illusion of hollow cheek. My hair was slicked into a smooth, dark cap. A series of slinky black evening gowns hung, like dark ghosts, on a metal rack. Once costumed, I looked like a bona fide member of the Addams family.

I tossed the skull back and forth with the midget; we sat at our picnic lunch, staring at the pork entree. I leaned against a black tree trunk in a dimly lit stone courtyard and for every shot, wore another silky black gown. *Réalités* loved the pictures! I, however, was somewhat chagrined when my aunt in Appleton, Wisconsin, who subscribed to the magazine, wrote to my parents about my unusual appearance. But, far worse, was my natural face without eyebrows—not the fresh, athletic look I wanted while skiing the mountains of Kitzbühel.

# 7

# The Fair Isle

Before leaving the Ryndam, Al, the Harvard graduate from the Bronx, and I had agreed to meet in Kitzbühel for Christmas skiing. It was his idea, not mine, since I had never heard of Kitzbühel. He traveled by train from London where he was studying at the London School of Economics and was waiting for me in Kitzbühel when my train arrived from Paris, in the middle of a huge snowstorm. As we piled into a horse-drawn sleigh, tunnels of wind-blown flakes circled through the air. The driver wrapped wool blankets around our knees and we headed for the pension where we both had rooms. My brother, who was stationed with the Army in Stuttgart, was scheduled to arrive the next day so we could put together the remnants of a family Christmas. Our pension, the Hannenkam, was tucked into a mountainside near the ski slopes at the end of a long, narrow, steep road. For five snowy days, the three of us skied the snow-packed Austrian trails, reveling in the Alpine climate and the warm, festive restaurants in Kitzbühel. On Christmas Eve we watched in solemn silence from the heights of the village as a procession of worshipers, each carrying a lighted candle, headed for mass in a beautiful white church in the valley below. That sight remains one of my more vivid memories of travel.

Unfortunately, Al's disappointing experience as a graduate student at the London School of Economics had led to a serious case of disenchantment with academic life. He had become cynically hedonistic and totally uninterested in studying. I thought he was wasting his talents and told him so. His reply: We should discuss this in bed. But not, I decided, in Austria.

I returned to Paris just after New Year's, but after all the physical freedom of a ski trip, I felt restless and cramped in my hotel room. There were no calls for fashion shoots, so in early January I impulsively decided to leave for London, a city in a country I had never seen. The boat trip across the Channel was miserable, with rough, choppy waves, and most of the passengers spent the cold trip throwing up while leaning over the railing on the deck. Yet the moment I stepped on dry land I knew I was home. What a relief to speak my native language again! My French was fluent by then but speaking that energetic language made me use facial muscles I didn't know I had. I happily relaxed my uvular "R," which I had recently perfected, and let the Anglo-Saxon tongue roll.

The kindness of the polite English took the edge off London's miserable weather. Al had thoughtfully arranged for dinner in a West End restaurant and bought theater tickets for my first night in the city. I was shocked by the poor quality of English food—slices of roast beef so thin they were transparent, bland winter vegetables and soggy potatoes. The dessert, a proper trifle, was overly sweet and messy. This was not a city for gourmets. The contrast with Paris in this respect was extreme. It was apparent everywhere that the English had had a much

more difficult time during the war than the French—and that
their recovery was slower and more arduous. The French, it
seemed, could put their love of creature comforts above their
love of country and freedom. Yet in London, I felt a warmth
and civility supported by a stoic, brave endurance that Paris,
as much as I loved its lifestyle, could never duplicate.

After the theater—an uproarious production of *The Taming
of the Shrew*, Shakespeare clearly articulated and brilliantly
performed—we emerged to empty winter streets. We stood for
nearly an hour in wet snowfall trying to hail a taxi. It was a
hopeless pursuit. In bitter cold weather, just when they were
needed most, London taxis would suddenly disappear. The few
cabs that rumbled by refused to stop, so our only option was to
begin walking down Piccadilly Street. The snow was blinding
us as we beat against the wind, our heads buried in our coat
collars wrapped with scarves. After half an hour, my feet were
wet and I was miserably cold. It was nearly one o'clock in the
morning. Just as I said that I couldn't walk another step, we
passed the entrance to the Carlisle Hotel. Impulsively, I turned
and went quickly inside, followed by Al.

The lobby was empty except for one corpulent gray-haired
man reading the *London Times* and drinking cognac in front
of the gas fireplace. His slouching posture suggested that the
cognac was only one of many he had consumed. As we sank
into the cushions of the couch directly across from him, he put
down his newspaper and said, peering over his reading glasses,
"Dreadful weather tonight," in a perfect upper class British
accent. "May I offer you something to drink?"

We were more than happy to accept his offer and warmed
ourselves with the amber liquid. "What brings you Americans

to London?" he asked. I explained that I lived in Paris and was visiting London for the first time. Then I added that I was in France to perfect my language skills and become a writer, ambitions only partially realized because of my new career as a fashion model. This intrigued our charming, self-appointed host. Al, as a graduate student at the London School of Economics, was apparently following an acceptable pursuit.

"And you, miss, are...?" "My name is Ann Montgomery," I replied. "I am Randolph Churchill," our new friend said, extending his hand. I stared at him in complete disbelief. Though I was reluctant to ask, I finally said, "Are you related to Winston Churchill?" I thought his famous name might possibly be only a coincidence. "Winston is my father" was the amazing answer. For a long moment, I was silent, a torrent of questions locked in my throat.

Mr. Churchill sipped the last of his cognac and closed the subject by inviting us to share his chauffeur-driven limousine. We sat in the back seat and Churchill beside the chauffeur, something Al insisted was never done. "I'm on my way to Annabelle's," he announced. "Won't you come with me?" I had never heard of the famous nightclub, of course. Al and I looked at each other and we both shook our heads. Randolph tried several times to persuade us, but I kept insisting that I had to return to my hotel since I was leaving for Paris early in the morning, another of my twists on the truth. I did wonder why a man of such peerage was alone, but I could not bring myself to take advantage of his invitation, because Al would necessarily be member of the part, and I wasn't sure that I wanted Al's company at that moment.

At one o'clock in the morning, Churchill had already been drinking for several hours, but he contained his notorious drunken temper and behaved with admirable reserve. He had recently divorced his first wife, Pamela Digby (in 1971 she would marry Averell Harriman). His second marriage, to June Osborne, was finished as well. When we refused his invitation, Churchill was quiet until we arrived at the club where he got out, saying, "Please, my dear, allow my driver to take you home," and left us in the charge of the chauffeur. I never did go to Annabelle's, a famous London club where one could rub noses with a lot of titled folk. Randolph went club crawling alone that night, and the gallant chauffeur drove Al and me to our respective lodgings.

London was a city with streets that let the traffic flow, in contrast to the overburdened arteries of Paris. Taxis—my preferred mode of transportation now that I was a successful model—could be captured at a moment's notice unless, of course, the weather turned cold and wet. Bad weather drove all taxis to secret shelters and I often waited half an hour or more for the rare black cab. If Paris was cold and windy, at least you could warm up indoors. Not in London. For some reason the British seemed to think it healthier to live in freezing rooms. Hands and feet were like ice while the face turned red from gas or coal heated fireplaces. In the fifties, Londoners still burned soft coal, which made the smog so thick in the winter that cars and people frequently had to creep around in foggy darkness, even at midday.

But there were aspects of London life that were highly desirable, not the least of which were the dozens of stores selling beautiful ready-to-wear clothes at bargain prices. Paris had nothing comparable—its *prêt-a-porter* boutiques were almost as expensive as the couture. The two cities seemed to complement each other in their endless contradictions. I was charmed by both and soon began to make frequent trips back and forth. Al, still depressed with student life, continued to be my escort. His latest decision was to chuck it all and go back to New York to make money as his father had. I didn't approve at all—a small indication of what a high-minded bohemian I had become.

Before I left the city, after my second trip in February, Al and I ended our day at the Tate Museum at his small apartment on Bromley Square. We each poured a glass of wine and settled down on the couch, trying to warm ourselves at the gas fireplace while discussing the amazing paintings by Constable and Turner we had seen. Al put his arm around me and pulled me closer. "This is the time for us," he said. He often insisted we should take our relationship to a more intimate level. "I don't know about that," I answered hesitantly. Something about him bothered me. On one level, I enjoyed our banter and companionship, but on another, I was uneasy. But, okay, I was finally persuaded. Partially undressed, we lay down on the bed, both of us hiding under the duvet. I turned toward him and was stunned by his teary eyes. "It's because I'm so much in love with you," he said, choking slightly. You are what? Nothing was going to happen; he was hopelessly impotent. I was instantly relieved of my need to please and it was suddenly clear that I had made a terrible mistake. Not only was I doing something I didn't want to do to "please," but instinct told me, too late, that I didn't know much about my friend Al. I dressed as quickly as possible and started for the door. Before we parted, he grabbed my hand and looking soulfully into my eyes said,

"I'm sorry. I should have told you long ago. I'm afraid I'm homosexual and was hoping you could change that for me." Running for the door, I couldn't get away fast enough.

In London I was fortunate to have a hard-bitten but solidly professional modeling agent named Jean Smith. I would arrive from Paris and within minutes, it seemed, she had set up a full week of shoots for me. I was introduced to Norman Parkinson, British *Vogue*'s famous fashion photographer and also the official photographer of the Queen and the British royal family; John French, an excellent fashion photographer who worked for *The Queen* and John Kubric at *Harper's Bazaar*. By May, I would be on the cover of *The Tatler* magazine, thanks to a beautiful color photo taken by John French. I had only to call Jean to announce my imminent arrival and she would book every free hour of my stay in London. My frequent trips to that orderly city were a great comfort and gave me some relief from the hectic Paris scene. I quickly established a strong reputation as a popular fashion model in London. In all respects, I owe that success to the brilliance of Norman Parkinson.

Norman was a gentleman of the old school—tall and slender, elegantly dressed in custom-tailored English suits, ironic and humorous—and blessed with a happy marriage to the beautiful Wenda, a former model. For more than a year, I was one of his favorite models. After a day of shooting in the country, we would go to a pub, Norman taking his whisky neat while tucking his hand into his pocket for a pinch of snuff. It was, he said, his favorite way to end the day—with strong drink, tobacco and a boiled egg. I could always make him laugh with my serious pronouncements about "life." I would talk about the importance of freedom and independence for women and he would let me know that what I really wanted was to be hopelessly bound to some suitable young man. He thought American girls were a marvel, "not only beautiful, but bright." When I finally introduced him to the love of my life, he took us both aside and said, "There is just one thing I want to tell you about marriage," he said solemnly. "Do not try to change each other. Don't try to make up who you are." It was wise counsel and at the time I remember thinking, rather piously, "But who would want to try to change another person?"

Norman was an excellent studio photographer but he much preferred to work outdoors, encouraging his models to help him create action pictures—walking, even running, posing as part of the environment. So he was understandably restless when *Vogue* insisted he photograph a series of spring coats indoors. Fretting at his confines, he was in an impatient mood. I was dressed in a bright pink mohair coat with an olive green felt hat that looked a little like something the Queen might wear. (The English are very fond of hats.) In my white-gloved hands, I held a perfect pink English rose. I sat on a bench for what seemed an extremely long time while Norman adjusted and readjusted the warm spotlights. The room was getting hotter. Beads of perspiration appeared on his face as he struggled for the best illumination. He was always a demanding perfectionist, but I found this endless fussing annoying, though of course, I was in no position to open my mouth. I was the object, not the subject. Photographing in color is always more exacting, and as I later wrote to a friend, "Posing for Mr. Parkinson requires more patience at times than I have." I was holding the requested pose, waiting for him to arrange the lighting, when I felt a slight wave of nausea. My chin dropped to my chest and I tumbled forward off the bench, falling to the floor, in a complete swoon. Under the hot lights and in an overheated room, I had suddenly fainted. While I was fighting for my vision and a clear head I was thinking, "So this is how real illness strikes—suddenly, without warning, leaving you in darkness." Fortunately, my introspection was far more dramatic than the reality.

As I lay curled on the floor, dazed and confused, I was still clutching the long-stem English rose in my white-gloved hand. Nonplussed by this interruption in his work, Norman said absolutely nothing once I revived, but he did help me back onto the bench. He held my shoulders with both hands, arranging them just as he wanted for the picture, literally propping me up, tilting my head as if I were a doll to get the proper angle. "Now," he said calmly, "please hold that pose." The photograph was suffused with a rosy glow, my pale face luminously peaceful. The whole thing left me with a hangover headache, but I did recover sufficiently to work two more hours while we finished the shoot—and *Vogue* was apparently thrilled with the result. On Wednesday, again with Mr. Parkinson, I posed for two hours underneath the London Bridge, in a chill rain swept by an even colder wind. Even in the warm camelhair coat I was modeling, I felt the bitter cold. On days when the weather was my enemy, as was often the case, I felt I had really earned the extravagant sum I was paid.

In late January, now back in Paris, I got an urgent call from Jean Smith. Louis Schurr, a famous Hollywood agent,

to England for Friday, Saturday and Sunday. "It seems I have been chosen as one of the *belles mannequins francaises* who will appear on an American television show starring Bob Hope and Kirk Douglas. I'll be paid $100.00 and all expenses—bravo! So, you will see your daughter's face on television (my parents had not seen me since I left Ohio several months before) grinning at one or both of the 'stars' involved."

My frequent trips to England always included agonizing interviews with the customs officials as I entered the country. I lied as often as I could, saying "Yes, I am a student and here as a tourist," then, rushing for the London train, would hurry to my agent's office for a list of appointments during my two week stay—the longest stay I would be allowed. I was relieved to be flying to London for the television show because first class travelers were never subjected to a grilling about the purpose of their visit.

For three days with the *Bob Hope Show*, I was Mademoiselle Ann, a French model, wearing an elegant strapless gown and stole, thickly embroidered with seed pearls and rhinestones, created by Pierre Balmain. Bob Hope, master of ceremonies, directed the rehearsals for the models, perfecting our roles in the fashion extravaganza. As the only member of the fashion cast who spoke English, I became the translator. Hope would give me directions and I would translate them into French for the other mannequins—who naturally detested me for my bilingual ability and the power it gave me. Moreover, I was the only one who understood his jokes. Kirk Douglas was strangely absent. I never saw him on the set.

During a break in the rehearsal, I went to the studio luncheonette for a sandwich and Hope's brother, Jack, followed me there, sitting beside me. "Bob would like to have you come by his room for a drink tonight," he said. I gazed at him quizzically, then, still trying to sort out the implications of this invitation, answered truthfully that I was meeting a friend after the rehearsal. In fact I was meeting a friend. Not easily discouraged, Jack began to give me a biographical tribute to his brother, explaining, "Bob is really a great guy. You'll enjoy being with him." And to further enlist my sympathies, he told me the story of Bob's poor, humble youth in Cleveland, Ohio. "He was a dead-end kid there," Jack explained. I was fascinated by this sketch of his youth. But if I could say no to Randolph Churchill, it wasn't that much harder to say no to Bob Hope. I would have liked him, I'm sure, but motivated by a mysterious yet undeniable anxiety, I was afraid of a close encounter.

The fabric of the strapless evening dress and padded stole I wore for the television show was encrusted with hundreds of hand-sewn seed pearls and rhinestones. With its jeweled embroidery, the stole rested heavily on my shoulders and it was with relief that I came down the ramp, unloaded the stole and swept off the stage in the matching gown.

Hope was at his peak of his popularity then, an adored comedian at the top of his game, where he would remain for the rest of his life. He had come a long way from his low-rent neighborhood in Cleveland. After the show ended, he lined up all the models, except me, and posed for several photographs with his arms around them. I stood watching from the edge of the stage, realizing I had been purposefully excluded. The lesson: You can't have it both ways. I had already made a choice that angered him.

During this trip to London, I said my final farewell to Al, but surprisingly, I had not heard the last of him. He began seeing a psychiatrist in London and went to Spain for his spring vacation. From there he reported that he was drunk for three solid weeks, promiscuously involved with a series of women and finally, thrown into jail for civil disobedience by Franco's Falangist police. He had won a coveted scholarship to Harvard graduate school, and then decided he didn't want it after all. At the somewhat late age of twenty-seven, he was still trying to find his real self. We never met again, but I always hoped that he finally decided in favor of graduate school at Harvard.

# Chez Chanel

The streets of Paris were coated with ice when I returned from London, having successfully created a second modeling career in that city. It was the worst month in one of the coldest winters ever recorded and Saint-Germain-des-Prés was windblown and empty. As I walked into the Hotel Welcome, Madame Guillies, the older, less attractive of the two blond sisters who managed the hotel, was fussing with some papers behind the reception desk. The moment she saw me, she began a rapid tirade, the pitch of her voice rising with each sentence. Fresh from speaking English for almost a month, I was baffled, understanding less than half what she said. Nothing made any sense, least of all her anger. After some careful questioning, the confusion cleared. In my absence, she had been deluged with an avalanche of phone calls from photographers and editors all over Paris who wanted me to model the spring collections. Some of the callers, she claimed, particularly the photographers, were rude, not that Madame wasn't a match for anyone's bad temper. She was outraged that I had left, telling no one where I was going.

After I had returned from the skiing vacation in Kitzbühel, my hotel room seemed small and dark. Paris was unusually quiet and freezing cold, and after the fun of Kitzbühel, I felt lonely and neglected. Heady with success and well-funded mobility, I had impulsively packed my suitcase and left wintry Paris for a foggy, rain-soaked London.

During my stay in London I was encouraged by an editor at British *Vogue* to get a modeling agent. She suggested Jean Smith, a thoroughly professional agent, and she was my first choice. Jean immediately began scheduling bookings and, eventually, collecting the money I had earned. These essential services for a freelance fashion model didn't exist in Paris. The ease of working in the British fashion scene was a great relief. I had several shoots with Norman Parkinson, the preeminent photographer of British *Vogue*. It was my first meeting with him and we would work together many times in the future. But this particular London junket was hopelessly wrong. I had abandoned Paris, the fashion capitol of the world, at the height of the spring collections. What kind of a fool was I? Once again, my chronically restless nature had led to disaster. My decision was prompted by my new persona—American girl in Paris, recent college graduate, modeling for the top fashion photographers and earning more money than she ever dreamed possible. That girl had a few lessons to learn. As a result of this miscalculation, I had fallen clumsily from my glamorous pedestal.

Before and during the collections, Santé Forlano, the top photographer French *Vogue* and Guy Arsac, one of the most successful freelance photographers, had called me frequently for photo shoots. They were furious that I had gone blissfully off to London while the spring collections were unveiled to the press.

# Chapter 8

Every fashion magazine in the western world was represented by top editors accompanied by photographers racing to record the work of the fabulous couturiers during the two-week blitz of showings. I was unaware that I was missing the first fashion event of 1955. But once back in Paris I realized my mistake. The collections were over, the fashion world quietly readying for another flurry of manic activity—the fall collections in August. And Paris was turning a bitterly cold shoulder to me. Among other gaffes, I had missed the opportunity to earn money I would need for the slow months ahead.

An angry Guy Arsac finally reached me. While I held the phone away from my ear, he loudly berated me for deserting the scene. He had planned to use me exclusively as his model for the collections. He naturally assumed that, after two months of frequent fashion shoots in his barn-like studio, I would be in Paris for the collections.

I didn't know where to begin to reinstate my modeling career in Paris, so I decided to apply for a position as a couture model. Once again I appealed to Marjorie Beck, who was surprised to hear from me. She found it hard to believe that I would abandon freelance photography modeling to work for one client, but she reluctantly agreed to introduce me to Coco Chanel.

On a chill but sunny March morning I left my taxi on the place de la Concorde and walked quickly to a ten o'clock appointment at Chanel's *maison de couture* on rue Cambon. The first floor was a glittering trove of square-cut perfume bottles—Chanel No. 5, the world's best-selling perfume, flanked by other scents: No. 22, Gardenia, Bois des Iles and Cuir de Russie. Coco's beautifully designed costume jewelry—large gem-studded brooches, the famous cuff bracelets set with precious and semiprecious stones, ropes of lustrous pearls interspersed or clasped with jewels—were arrayed in brass-trimmed glass cases. Shelves of her signature handbags were encased behind glass doors. Even at high noon few shafts of sunlight penetrated the narrow rue Cambon, heavily shadowed as it was by the Ritz Hotel. But the elegant interior was bathed in spotlights that gave it an Oz-like glow.

When I arrived, a young woman, elegantly dressed in a simple black shift, escorted me up the curving stairs, luminously lined with mirrors, to the second floor salon. The room was empty except for two dozen gilt-painted faux bamboo chairs, arranged on the plush beige carpet before the small raised platform where collections were presented.

The stairway continued to the third floor where, I would learn, the door to Chanel's private apartment was covered in the same gray suede as its wall, nearly invisible to the casual eye. Company offices—public relations, accounting and purchasing—shared the third floor. Above this, at the top of a narrow staircase, were the ateliers where the seamstresses labored. In those rooms, barely heated in winter and stifling hot in the summer, skilled hands encrusted silk with hundreds of tiny seed pearls and rhinestone beads, pieced handmade lace panels into chiffon, covered buttons for discreet custom buttonholes with invisible stitches. The seamstress culture was hierarchical, with the most experienced dressmakers instructing and quietly observing as the youngest learned their skills. They were justifiably proud of their craft, which was carefully passed on from one generation to the next—often within the same family, from mother to daughter. When collections were being prepared, the mannequins would climb those stairs to be fitted with a muslin pattern, the first step in creating a new costume.

As I settled into a chair to wait, Chanel herself was not visible, but she could see me. It was her habit to stand or sit at the top of the carpeted circular stairway where the activity in the salon was reflected in the mirror-lined wall beside her. From this vantage point, she would watch the audience's reactions when her collections were presented. It also allowed her to make an assessment of my appearance before we even met.

Finally Coco came slowly down the curving staircase and quietly entered the salon. Though she was barely over five feet tall, I found her presence formidable and almost frightening. She was a miniature, sturdy sylph—an alert, tiny bird (my private name for her was *le petit oiseau*), with movements both quick and wary. That day she was wearing a softly tailored black suit—a color she usually wore—with a white silk blouse, its cuffs folded over the suit's sleeve. She was never without her signature rope of pearls or the brilliantly jeweled costume brooches she designed. A small pillbox hat, also black, perched on her head, its half veil emphasizing her dark eyes, darting, alert and observant. Her expression was wise and guarded—it seemed to say, this world cannot always be trusted and it must be watched

Chanel's first name, Coco, was actually taken from a song she sang, "Ko Ko Ri Ko," when she flirted with being an entertainer in the cafés of Deauville. After her mother died when Coco was still a young girl, her itinerant, feckless father left her and her sister in an orphanage, where she was raised and given a strict convent education—including learning the seamstress trade. Gabrielle was her given name, but it was "Coco" that stayed with her.

Before I had made the appointment with Chanel, I had been "interviewed" (though never by the couturier himself) by Dior, Jacques Fath and Balmain, all of whom found me wrong for their designs. I was too tall, too thin—or, in the case of Dior—not thin enough. A fitter had put me into one of his luxurious evening gowns but she couldn't budge the back zipper. In that case, my rib cage was the problem. But the meeting with Chanel was well timed. Her *demi-collection* was scheduled for May 5 (five was her lucky number)—after the January spring couture showings and before those of the winter in late summer. Since she had already decided to hire an additional model for that fashion event, there was a place for me.

Because Chanel refused to allow anyone to write about her life until after she died, I had no way of knowing her amazing and fascinating history. Her many male lovers were legendary and always wealthy. A long liaison with the Duke of Westminster had placed her in the ranks of high society in both London and Paris. With her intelligence and wit, elegant soirees in Paris and London revolved around her. As part of a sophisticated and successful artistic crowd in Paris, she had designed costumes for a Jean Cocteau ballet.

Because her English was more fluent than my still some-what hesitant French, we easily negotiated the terms of my three-month contract. My only request was that I be allowed to continue fashion shoots when I was not showing her collection. I was shocked to discover the small salary paid to house models. It would be financially essential for me to keep working as a photographer's model and in any case, I had no intention of giving it up to become a dressmaker's dummy. Coco was seventy-one, with the energy and creativity of a much younger woman. I was twenty-two and just beginning my young adult life. We had very little in common. I was escaping a claustrophobic small Ohio town. Chanel was both wealthy and worldly, an artist and a shrewd businesswoman with a flair for personal candor. She had a steely power that drove her success, but I found her studied intelligence and perceptive opinions very appealing. I felt triumphant to be accepted as a model for the new collection.

Before the war, Chanel had made millions of dollars from the designs that bore her label and from Chanel No. 5, the extremely successful perfume that she created by cleverly mixing several natural scents to make its spicy, sweet aroma. She secured her personal wealth by selling two thirds of the thriving perfume business to the Wetrheimer family. In 1939, during the German occupation of Paris, the couture world quietly died and she reluctantly closed her salon, though she kept the *parfumerie* on the first floor open. Once the war ended, she found retirement boring and convinced the Wertheimers to finance the reopening of her *maison de couture*.

The first postwar Chanel collection in February of 1954 heralded her return, but the Paris fashion press greeted it with disdain. The simple, wearable designs were rejected as retro, a return to the jaded style of the nineteen twenties, offering no challenge to the preeminence of Christian Dior's New Look. His opulent costumes made lavish use of fabric—padded, flared and fur trimmed garments celebrating the end of wartime scarcity. Jacques Fath and Pierre Balmain followed his lead with the extravagant designs that were welcomed by women customers worldwide. Mass marketing was making its appearance in the fashion world and fortunes would be made from the copies of couture clothing. The press focused the world's attention on Paris, making it once more the center of the fashion universe.

Once my contract was signed, I entered the "dollhouse," as I called the *cabine,* the small room with walls of mirrors above the makeup shelves where the models were closeted. There were two doors, one to the room where the collection was kept and a heavy door to the salon, padded with red velvet,that was always closed. More gilt chairs matching those in the main salon were stationed in front of the makeup counter. *Les mannequins* were confined to this room when not presenting the collection or showing designs to clients. In repose, they sat before their mirrors, endlessly applying and reapplying their makeup. With a tiny makeup brush, they carefully redefined the lines of black mascara to exaggerate the size of their eyes, outlining their lips in purple, coating them again and again with deep pink lipstick. With a slight frown, they would purse their lips, sucking in their cheeks to emphasize cheekbones, never once averting their eyes from the mirror. Living dolls, endlessly painting themselves, hoping to create a miraculous change of face. The room was ruled, I would discover, by the iron hand of Madame Lucie, who dictated when we were to arrive and leave. No one moved without her permission and she seemed to have a special relationship with Chanel. Years later, rumors confirmed the unbelievable fact that she too was one of Coco's lovers.

Each model was given a "merry widow" underwire bustier. This novel Victorian garment cinched the waist and plumped the bosom and was required by Chanel. "I want mannequins with bosoms and hips," she insisted. "Today's look is the elegance of the cemetery. It makes women look like ghosts." Over that we wore a short silk robe that tied in front like a kimono. Silk underwear, stockings with garter belt (pantyhose had yet to be invented) and a half-slip completed the ensemble. Within hours, on my first day, I wanted to escape the regimented, airless scene of this new fashion frontier. From the moment I stepped inside, I could feel my self-confidence weaken. I had traded my independence for more than the loss of freedom. In this closeted environment I was quite simply bored to death.

The other models seemed content to sit studying their faces and gossiping about their amorous affairs. Fascinated with their reflections, they constantly checked their image, to make sure, I thought, that it didn't evaporate. Imagine Narcissus without his pond! Madame Lucie was a portly older woman with bleached hair. She was heavy-handed, rude and controlling. Her role as *chef de cabine* was to make sure the models were prepared to show the collection every day at one o'clock and that they arrived and departed on time. She decided which models were patronized as "favorites" of Mademoiselle Chanel, those most frequently asked to show customers the collection. I hated the "live mannequin" part of the couture business and although I was initially in demand for showings, I made it clear I didn't want to wear the clothes for buyers and bluntly refused to cooperate. In addition, Madame Lucie and I had serious disagreements about the time clock. I simply refused to arrive or leave on schedule.

Chanel, famous for her fashion maxims, once said, "Real elegance means elegance in manners, too. Look at women—how they take out boxes of makeup and put them on the table, applying makeup in public. How can one be elegant doing this? And all those women who leave lipstick all over table napkins and on glasses! I tell them my table linen is too fine to be spoilt by you." One wonders what she thought of her models' tireless primping.

Shortly after I began my work as a mannequin at Chanel's, I was called for a fitting of a new design—a bias cut, sheer black chiffon cocktail dress with lace trim. Chanel was in the salon, sitting on one of the gilt chairs, and motioned for me to come stand before her. She never drew her designs, but created everything by working with the fabric itself, draping it so the seamstresses could recreate her vision. Both Madame Lucie and the head seamstress stood beside her. I was already in a quiet rage since I loathed being fitted, forced to stand motionless while pins were shoved into my body like I was a stuffed effigy. Guarded by her seamstress, Chanel was quiet while the fitting proceeded, directing it with incisive comments followed by instructions about the drape or cut of the dress. It took all my self-control to stand still as a statue while I wanted to scream, "Don't touch me!"

Chanel peered closely at the dress, saying that the flow of the skirt was not right. As she reached forward, tugging at the material of the skirt, indicating that she wanted it to fall at an angle, not a straight line, my momentary trance was broken and with a sudden jerk, I stepped back, out of reach—a completely involuntary movement. I could hear a quick intake of breath as Madame Lucie registered her disapproval. The embarrassed seamstress kept her eyes glued to the floor, terrified of Chanel's reaction. After several moments of silence, Chanel said to the assemblage, "Mademoiselle Ann *est fatiguée aujourd'hui.*" Mademoiselle Ann is tired today. For the moment, I was saved—and effectively forgiven. Chanel had chosen not to display her notorious temper. The fitting was completed the next day in the seamstress' atelier and the dress was one of the hits of that collection.

Behind Chanel's fashion clairvoyance lay her simple belief that a perfectly constructed suit or dress should flow with the natural lines of the figure. This philosophy would become the foundation of her wearable styles for women of the late twentieth century and beyond.. She abandoned pretense for simplicity, artifice for art. From a career that began with a hat shop in Deauville when she was barely twenty, she built a fashion empire that brought her wealth and fame by the time she was in her early thirties. The elegance of her collections was legendary. Unfortunately, though I was deeply impressed by her extraordinary business skills, I found it increasingly difficult to endure the tedious routines of the *cabine*. I had joined it reluctantly and was still grieving for my freelance life.

Being forced to sit in the small, mirrored room for six hours each day made me restless and claustrophobic. I was bored by the tedium and inactivity. Besides, I desperately wanted to distance myself from the depressing lives of the other models— their fear of aging eased only by the hope of becoming some man's *petite maîtresse* before it was too late.

To escape, I read constantly. The novels of Henry James— with portraits of wealthy, privileged continental travelers and expatriates—were particularly comforting. I wish I had a photograph of myself, laced into the merry widow, robed in a white silk kimono, hunched over the fine print of *Portrait of a Lady*. I could see that the European models had few hopes for the future beyond the cheerless one of becoming too old to find work. Spending my days in the *cabine* was not what I had in mind. I was beginning to fear losing my identity as an adventurous American girl, future unknown. Perhaps this had already happened.

Marjorie Beck had occasional photo shoots but I was the only *Vogue* model. Two of the mannequins, Juditte and Maria, were refugees from Communist Hungary, living in Paris, as they would frequently tell you, more from necessity than desire. Both were handsome, striking Slavic beauties. Maria, Juditte and Juditte's husband, Robert, were Marjorie and her husband Christopher's close friends. "You know," Maria would say imperiously, "I am a Hungarian countess." The lilt of her accented English gave this confession the desired touch of drama. She never held forth on any subject without mentioning her title, except when she was holding your hand in hers, reading your fortune in a hushed voice. A bit of the gypsy in that countess, I thought. Juditte was the more sophisticated of the two and claimed to be an undiscovered talent (she was writing an opera). She was fond of recounting embellished tales of her former life in Budapest, insisting that it was far more exciting than *la gaîté parisienne*.

Maria, Marjorie and Juditte gossiped for hours, trying to outdo each other with tales of their evening debacles, punctuated by loud laughter. They particularly enjoyed sharing details of drinking and sexual encounters on their nightly forays to the cafés and bars of the Left Bank. They had black circles of fatigue under their eyes and endless headaches from over-indulgence. More than once both Juditte and Maria appeared with fresh purple bruises or cuts on their lips that had to be frantically camouflaged with makeup. I endured the babble for a couple of days and then decided to protect myself with the only armor I had, withdrawal. While they prattled on with their attempts to shock, I buried my head in another place, the Europe of Henry James: the perfect escape.

One week after I began at Chanel's, Marjorie left the *cabine* during her lunch break and never returned. She called to say she was ill. In actuality, she, Christopher, Juditte, and Robert had been out drinking the night before. All kinds of passions were inflamed and Juditte's husband left the three revelers in disgust. This created an opportunity for Juditte, Marjorie and Christopher to stagger drunkenly into a Left Bank hotel room and spend the night, a thoroughly inebriated troika. Marjorie ended up with a badly discolored bruised eye. In the morning, when she discovered Juditte and Christopher in bed together, she stalked out of the room and out of his life. When I met Christopher the next night at the Café Flore, at his request, for an aperitif, he admitted that Marjorie had left him and gone to join her former husband, Fred Beck, in the Canary Islands. Christopher, a Left Bank poet of modest reputation, seemed rather sanguine about it all, saying *"Eh bien, tant pis,"* something the French were forever uttering with a shrug. "Oh, well, too bad." I was mystified by his cynicism. Within three months, Christopher and Juditte, already pregnant with his child, would move to Majorca, where they eventually married.

At noon on May 5, the *prevue* of Chanel's new demi-collection was ready for the fashion press. Coco parted the curtains behind the platform, anxiously surveying the sparsely filled semicircle of gilt chairs. The room was bathed in soft overhead lights, the beige carpet smooth as a velvet glove. Just before the appointed hour, the murmured conversations of the audience began to break the expectant hush. Chanel retired to her hidden perch at the top of the mirrored stairway to watch the reactions. She had hoped for better attendance, but the fashion elite stayed away in droves, avoiding what they assumed would be another parade of dated fashions.

Coco's reputation was also hampered by suspicions that she had compromised her French patriotism by her wartime love affair with Hans von Dincklage, a German general and a spy. There were rumors that she was a collaborator. There is, in fact, evidence that she tried to persuade her friend Winston Churchill to sign an armistice with the Germans before the war's end. As history tells us, he wisely refused. This was treasonable action on Chanel's part. Were it not for the fact that Churchill sent a car at night so she could escape to Switzerland as the German occupation ended, she would probably have been dragged through the streets of Paris and jailed as a traitor. Perhaps she was a collaborator and certainly right wing, but we never talked politics. I always thought her allegiance was more to herself than any political ideology.

At the final rehearsal for the *defilade,* as the collection presentation was called, Chanel had been upset and very critical. She lectured the models, saying they looked sad. I was the only exception, she insisted, and instructed the other models to apply their lipstick as I did, which made me distinctly unpopular. It was not my lipstick that set me apart, of course, but the shape of my mouth and the practiced vestige of a smile that I often wore for photos. Smiling was not part of the couture mannequin's mien. It seemed that smiles detracted from the clothes being shown. We slouched and pouted. Coco had taught us how to walk— demonstrating herself the gliding gait with hips thrust forward, shoulders tilted back, level turns with hand on hip—a plausible imitation of the debutante slouch so popular in the twenties.

# Chapter 8

Chanel, as anxious as a playwright on opening night, was obviously distressed by the sparse attendance of fashion journalists, too many of whom were conspicuously absent. I recognized only Francoise de Langlade, the fashion editor of *Vogue*, poised to write in her black notebook. Once the presentation began, Chanel sat in her hidden spot at the top of the stairs where she could safely observe the reactions, reflected in the mirrors, while unseen by the audience.

As I stood, costumed and waiting for my first appearance, Chanel pinned a silk gardenia, her favorite flower, on my shoulder. No outfit of hers was complete without a flower or ropes of satiny pearls. I carried a small card, printed with the number of the suit, in my right hand. With my left hand modishly resting on my hipbone, I walked to the center of the stage, wearing a classic Chanel suit in ivory wool bouclé, its hip-length jacket trimmed in black and closed at the neck with jet black buttons. I hesitated for a moment, removing the jacket to reveal a white silk blouse with its soft bow at the neck. As I made my turns on the small stage, the audience, finally alert, shifted in their gilt chairs with an audible rustle. I sauntered stage left, gliding slowly in the Chanel sling-back pumps (ivory leather, patent toe), made a half turn and glided stage right, hips thrust forward, toes out, a modish ballerina with a half smile on my face, ending with a pirouette at the center and exiting stage right. Applause burst forth.

That Chanel suit would become a fashion legend, though the French press still reserved its highest praise for Dior, Jacques Fath and Balmain. The suit's graceful cut, following rather than restructuring the female form, was dismissed as inferior to the elaborate costumes of the New Look. But Louise Dahl-Wolfe, the editor of American *Vogue*, was immediately taken with its simple lines and look of comfortable elegance. That this now famous piece of clothing could dominate the fashion scene for decades would have surprised everyone, including Coco herself. Her classic suit became a worldwide symbol of elegance. Her success would revive Chanel's past triumphs in the minds of the fashion journalists and her renaissance as a trendsetter in the vanguard of haute couture was assured.

When the show ended and the last of the lingering press had given Chanel their congratulations, she asked to see me. We were alone in the small hallway just outside the *cabine,* where the other models couldn't hear our conversation. She was obviously pleased with the reception of her collection. She had been courageous enough to challenge the other couturiers with her own new look. She told me that Francoise de Langlade, the fashion editor of *Vogue,* had come to her and complimented her on her new model, Mlle. Ann, as I was called, saying she intended to hire me as the *prêt-a-porter* model for *Vogue*'s 1955 Fall Collection issue. Then Chanel added some praise of her own, saying how much I had done to make the collection a success with my perfect carriage and graceful walk. Her compliments were very reassuring. My first few months of modeling in Paris had been exciting but I often felt like an outsider. Of course, being an outsider was a role I both cherished and nurtured because it made me feel, mistakenly, more secure. But, once a Chanel model, I was no longer a stand-in, but an actor on the fashion stage.

As the new model in the Chanel collection, I got a flurry of phone calls. Once again I was in demand for fashion shoots. Chanel and I had agreed that I would be allowed to continue my career as a fashion photographer's model, but the rules of life in the *cabine* were never clearly defined. That was left to the tough-minded Madame Lucie. After the opening, we continued to present the full collections for buyers and a few stragglers of the fashion press each day at one o'clock. When this was finished, I was—theoretically—free to leave for photo assignments and, on one particular day, an appointment with Santé Forlano at *Vogue*.

As I was about to leave, my case of makeup and shoes in hand, I was stunned to see Madame Lucie blocking my passage with her stiffly corseted girth. "*Ou allez-vous, Mademoiselle Ann?*" she demanded. I explained that I had an appointment for a fashion shoot at *Vogue*. She, physically standing her ground, said, "*Non. C'est interdite!*" It's forbidden! It was useless to say that Chanel herself had given me permission for photo appointments, because Madame Lucie was in charge. She was not going to let me out of my trapped existence in the *cabine* because, as she announced, it disturbed the routine of the other mannequins. And it disturbed her. I was appalled at her rudeness, but determined to proceed. I stepped nimbly around her towering figure and fled down the stairs like Cinderella, out the door and onto the rue Cambon.

From that day on, my very presence enraged Madame Lucie. Someone once told me she and Chanel were lovers. What an absurd idea! She was an overweight, heavily powdered and rouged woman whose towering rage was her only distinguishing characteristic. Coco was known not only for her right wing politics but for her long list of male lovers and a woman or two as well. Still, I doubted if her roster of amorous liaisons included such and unattractive, aging matron. However, since no one at Chanel's ever broached the subjects of politics or sex, the truth was a highly kept secret. Chanel was known for her

acid sarcasm but I was never the victim of her barbed tongue.
With me, she was gracious and complimentary, always a wise
observer but never unkind. I still believe it was a rare privilege
to work with a master in the art of couture, an inspired and
gifted designer who thought nothing of taking on the fashion
world at seventy-one and staging her own comeback.

There were several weeks left of my three-month contract. But
with Madame Lucie now an enemy, I knew I had to leave—and
quickly. When I told Madame Lucie I was going to cancel my
contract, she looked frightened and immediately hurried up the
stairs to Coco's apartment to give her the news.

A few moments later, she told me imperiously that
Mademoiselle Chanel wanted to see me. Though she had a
beautiful suite at the Ritz Hotel where she slept every night, it
was in her apartment on the third floor of the couture house
that she entertained her friends with cocktails and dinner. It
was there that her exquisite personal taste was most accurately
reflected. As I entered the room, she was sitting on the pale
chocolate suede couch in a characteristic pose, her body tucked
into a corner of the couch, her right hand arched, holding an
English cigarette in a black holder. She was wearing one of
her suits, a pale pink bouclé with navy blue trim and ropes of
pearls covering the neck of a simple blouse. A small-brimmed
navy blue hat completed the ensemble. Behind the couch were
floor-to-ceiling bookshelves, filled with leather-bound volumes,
framed photos and objets d'art. A photograph of the Duke of
Westminster in his polo outfit was prominently displayed on
a round table beside the couch. He was not only her lover for
three intense years but also her lifelong friend. Two enormous
Chinese Coromandel screens, the beautifully lacquered designs

inlaid with mother-of-pearl veneer, flanked the bookshelves. On the glass coffee table, inlaid with marbleized swirls of gilt, was a pair of engraved silver boxes lined in gold, the duke's gifts to a younger Coco. The gold lining symbolized, as he told her, her inner self—strength of character and intelligence, her most precious assets. He understood her well. The room had a sumptuous aura, more evidence of this woman's impeccable taste.

"Sit down, please," she said, gesturing to one of the Louis Quatorze leather armchairs beside the couch. I felt like Alice in Wonderland after drinking the potion, my large head wobbling on my thin neck, my body slumped awkwardly in the chair. Coco chose to communicate in English, perhaps to erase one of the barriers between us. To my astonishment, there was nothing menacing in her manner.

She began with a few compliments about my healthy "American beauty" look, the modish persona I projected that had helped launch her successful collection. "The bouclé suit was as perfect on you as the black chiffon evening dress." She moved to the edge of the couch, her chin thrust forward, resting on her uplifted hand, watching me with her piercing dark eyes. "Tell me, mademoiselle, what do you plan to do when you can no longer model?" I looked at her in surprise, having anticipated an angry reproof for breaking my contract or a lecture on personal dishonesty. I didn't expect to be treated as her conversational equal. "Because," she continued, "you know it does not last, this youth and beauty." I listened carefully, still too self-conscious to make a coherent reply. I was being offered advice from this woman who was a self-made millionaire by the time she was in her thirties and whose creative genius had made her a legend. "Suzy Parker, the American model, is a true friend of mine, you know," she continued. "She is a very smart young woman—and a very successful model—and she is training herself to be a fashion photographer." I recalled the photo shoot I had glimpsed at *Elle* magazine: Suzy posing, poised and professional, a camera-perfect subject. There was an American girl who knew how to take care of her own future. Did I? Once, when Chanel was complimented on her attractive models, she replied sardonically, "Yes, my girls are pretty, and that's why they do the job. If they had any brains, they'd stop doing it." It was flattering to imagine that my rebellious behavior may have made her suspect that I had some brains. It was unusual to hear someone from the fashion world talk about ephemeral beauty. Fashion was, after all, created for women *d'un certain age*, rich enough to indulge a desire for eternal youth.

Chanel seemed determined to give me the benefit of her experience: "What do you want to do with your life?" she repeated pointedly, lighting another cigarette.

I replied that I had come to Paris hoping to pursue a career as a writer, but I had become a fashion model instead. I don't know why, but I felt that it would be demeaning to admit that I needed to be financially independent. She asked what kind of writing I wanted to do: a question I found difficult to answer, thinking of my failed attempts to sell my short stories. I suggested fashion journalism. This seemed to please her, and she reached into a drawer and pulled out a small blue cloth-bound volume. "This is my book," she said proudly, handing me a notebook filled with her fashion maxims. Her biographers and even her friends swear that she never wrote a word. But if she hadn't written the maxims in that volume, whoever did was not getting any credit that day. In that moment, as I thumbed through the small light blue volume with its perfect convent script, I believed it was her book. I was impressed and flattered that she had shown it to me. Chanel spoke to me as if she understood how dehumanizing modeling could sometimes be. Like secret collaborators, we met briefly on common ground as risk takers.

The press frequently quoted Coco's maxims, her witty commentaries on the fashion scene and human behavior. In *Vogue* (February 15, 1954) on the eve of her first collection after the war, she predicted her own future success, telling Axel Madsen, "I will dress thousands of women. I will start with a collection, the same size collection I used to make. About one hundred things, because I must start this way. It won't be a revolution, it won't be shocking. Changes must not be brutal, must not be made all of a sudden. The eye must be given time to adapt itself to a new thought. It will be a collection made by a woman with love. I make women look pretty and young...I find that men have better taste and judgment about clothes than women. When I want an opinion about what I have done, I ask some men friends to come in and tell me what they think; not professionals in the couture, just friends. I value their reactions much more than women's. Women should always bring a man with them in choosing dresses; a woman friend will probably give an insincere opinion. The man can be trusted."

The phenomenal success that began with her May collection was an affirmation of both talent and hard work. It was her work as a couturier that was absolutely essential to her existence. Once again she had rebuilt her career. To quote Coco herself, "How many cares one loses when one decides not to be something but to be someone."

Chanel's name was returned to its proper place of prominence, but it was not until 1957 that American *Vogue* and its editor Louise Dahl-Wolfe began to feature Coco's couture clothing in the editorial pages. Her renaissance as a designer was not complete until the 1960s. She was clairvoyant about trends in fashion, with a sure sense of how women wanted to dress. She believed the business of fashion was to be responsive to the ever-changing interactions of people and events.

Coco's predictions about fashion's future—simple, wearable designs, each detail, tuck or drape constructed with precision—reflected the lifestyles of contemporary women who were increasingly athletic, assertive and independent. "Clutter is necessary in a room, unnecessary in clothes," she said. Many of her greatest innovations in style came from men's clothing—turtleneck sweaters, tailored shirts and sailor hats from the boatmen in Deauville, slacks for informal wear, and evening pajamas were only a few of her ideas. She was as cosmopolitan as her creations—the bouclé wool suit with its bordered jacket barely touching the hipbone, the silk spectator sport dress so elegantly worn by the international set, the bias cut sheer silk chiffon evening wear that floated like butterfly wings with each move of its wearer. The ropes of pearls—long and short, collars of pearls trapped around the neck by jeweled clasps, clipped on earlobes, draped across bosoms—were ingeniously crafted of the real and fake. For all the flair, there was never a tailor's stitch amiss in her designs. Perfectly constructed, her creations have outlasted their designer, both in image and durability.

"A dress should not be a disguise," she had said. "If a fashion isn't taken up and worn by everybody, then it is not a fashion but an eccentricity, a fancy dress. An eccentric dress does not make one an eccentric—a woman is dull in an eccentric dress if she is dull without it. A dress must be made like a watch or the dress is over. A dress isn't right if it is uncomfortable. Nothing shows age more than the upper arms. Cover them. A dress must function; place the pockets accurately for use, never a button without a buttonhole. A sleeve isn't right unless the arm lifts easily." And finally, "Elegance in clothes means freedom to move freely".

As Chanel has become a fashion icon, I, one of her former *mannequins*, have become an artifact. I was her "Amerluk," the quaint French argot for expatriate Americans in the fifties.

# City of Light

While I was in London in the spring, Barbara and her friend, Lois Dickert, another journalist, found a spacious, charming apartment on the Quai Voltaire, with front windows that commanded a long view of the Seine. I felt abandoned in my shabby room at the Hotel Welcome, painfully envious of Barbara's newfound comfort. I traveled to London so frequently, however, that I reassured myself with the thought that an apartment would be too much responsibility and expense. Until June, Susan would remain on the top floor, so I wasn't completely alone.

Lois was a journalist, hired by *Time* magazine as a researcher, cleverly circumventing the embargo against women writers by filing stories from the Paris bureau. Years later she became *People* magazine's Hollywood gossip columnist in Los Angeles, a latter-day Hedda Hopper, complete with the large-brimmed black hat that was Hedda's signature.

The first time I visited their apartment, a sublet, we ate in the owner's studio. He was a Greek ceramist and his boldly crafted art moderne ceramic plates, tiles and jugs graced every surface. Large double glass doors opened onto a cool, verdant terrace with lush trailing grapevines, where we sipped our aperitif accompanied by pungent olives from Provence. Barbara joined us for dinner but, with a writing assignment due the next day, she retired early. Lois and I were left to indulge in a slightly inebriated heart-to-heart. She wanted to talk about the yearlong affair with her French lover, a married man, that had just ended tragically. He and his wife, a woman who looked older than he did and wore a funny flat hat perched on her permed gray curls, began to dine together in the same bistros where he had romanced Lois. She must have known about her husband's infidelity and was trying valiantly to win him back. The competition was tough. Lois was not a raving beauty, but her winsome, heart-shaped face was framed by long, red-gold hair, and she had youth in her favor. In addition, she had an independent life, very appealing to a man tied to a homespun wife. It was an established pattern in the French bourgeois marriage for the husband to have a *petite amie* or *une maitresse* on the side, though it obviously caused as much pain as adultery did in America. To no one's surprise, when the Frenchman rejected Lois, he returned to his wife. Each time she spoke his name, her eyes filled with tears.

I was suffering, quite differently, from a slowly eroding sense of self-worth. In the fashion world, rejection or acceptance was granted by the ephemeral nature of my physical appearance, something I couldn't control. Modeling could simultaneously create a sense of self-aggrandizement and of self-degradation. It was tempting to imagine a life sustained by money earned for beauty, an accident of nature, and to settle for that equation. I was still too young to worry about aging, but I felt threatened by the more tangible fear that my beauty (my uniqueness, my inner self even) could become *démodé* and discarded like last season's gown as a useless commodity. Then what would become of the would-be writer who had first come to Paris?

As I expressed my dilemma, Lois looked at me incredulously. She was adamant that I should forget my longing to become a journalist (she'd been there, done that) and if I could make twenty dollars an hour posing for fashion photos, I should accept my good fortune. "You know," she added for emphasis, "you've been making so much money for so long that you've forgotten what it's like to be poor." By that time in the evening, my perceptions were beginning to lack clarity and I sounded like a whiner, even to myself. Her argument was so rational and forcefully presented that I promised myself I would stop complaining and put more time and energy into my modeling career.

The mythic beauty of Paris in April is a cliché, yet the most jaded traveler is still seduced. In 1955, a winter of record-breaking cold had been followed by a bleak and rainy March and we began to think that spring would never come.

To escape the city, Barbara, Lois and I decided to go to Deauville, a resort town on the coast of Normandy, for the last weekend in March. The weather was certain to be almost as cold and blustery as it was in Paris, but at least we would be in the sea air. My modeling assignments seemed tedious and boring, and I needed a change. After more than half a year of living with the excitement of sudden success in the fashion world of Paris, I was coming perilously close to burnout. If I crashed, there was no cushion to break my fall. What had been thrilling and challenging—promising, it seemed, to change my life—had lost its luster. I was reverting to a familiar state of eternal longing. The world that only a few weeks before had been so full and welcoming had turned empty and gray.

Our hotel in Deauville, a former chateau, was ponderous and dreary. After one lackluster meal in the heavily draped dining room, I was ready to return to Paris. Barbara and Lois tried to persuade me to join them for an evening of disco music in the hotel bar and they were angry with me for refusing to join them in their foray to "meet some men." But I was intractable. In a sullen mood, I retreated to my room. After packing my small suitcase and asking the concierge to wake me at 7 a.m., I went quickly to sleep. Immediately after breakfast, I took the first train back to Paris.

My train pulled into the Gare du Nord just as the sun was coming out from behind a cover of morning clouds. I was pleasantly surprised to find a Paris basking in the first warm day in over six months. April was opening with a burst of brilliant sunshine and white chestnut blossoms.

When I returned to the Hotel Welcome a telegram from my brother was waiting for me. Uncertain about his future when he graduated from high school, he had impulsively decided to join the Army. This decision would work well for him in the long term, since it ultimately paid for his college education. But as the telegram indicated, the beginning of his Army career had been a little rocky. After basic training at Fort Knox in Kentucky, he was shipped to Stuttgart, Germany. On the troop ship, he had unwisely played poker with his sergeant and lost a lot of money. The sergeant was threatening to put him in the brig if he didn't come up with the cash—immediately. It was one of those "Send money quick" emergencies.

# Chapter 9

As I headed up the stairs to my room, my brother's telegram
in hand, two beaming young men leaned over the stair rail.
They too were part of spring. The winter term at England's
Oxford University, which they attended as American Rhodes
Scholars, had ended two weeks earlier and they had been staying
in the Hotel Welcome, spending their spring "vac" relaxing and
sightseeing in Paris. We had exchanged greetings before, but
I didn't know their names. "We're on our way to lunch," Al
Utton said. "Why don't you come with us?" I put my suitcase in
my room, delighted to have company for the meal and, my low
spirits finally lifting a little, strolled along the sunny Boulevard
Saint-Germain with Al and his friend, Jack Lymon.

We sat down under the budding trees on the sunny terrace
of a small bistro tucked into a narrow side street just off the
Boulevard Saint-Germain. The hovering shadows of my future
evaporated in the warm air. Jack would become a famous
heart surgeon in California and Allen, a lawyer, practicing
and teaching in New Mexico and serving as a strong state
leader for the Democratic Party. My invisible shadow might
have shown a graduate student in comparative literature,
poring over her books in a cold library at Northwestern
University, supported by a fellowship arranged by Professor
Irvin. But the magic of the day completely banished that
vision. Submerged in the perfection of the present moment,
we had a wonderful, funny conversation about our various
expatriate experiences. I agreed to get Jack and another friend,
Tom Blackburn, tickets to attend the couture show at Chanel.
As he earnestly explained, his mother would be fascinated
to hear that he had actually seen the spring collection of a
famous *maison de couture*.

We had a delicious leek and potato soup, a platter of cheeses with slices of French bread and fresh fruit for dessert. "Next stop is for coffee," Jack announced and, still euphoric from the balmy air that had transformed the quartier, I quickly agreed.

The Café Mabillon was around the corner on the boulevard. Chairs and round tables had been placed on the sidewalk, the heavy winter awning rolled away. The faintest shadow of leafing trees was just beginning to make patterns on the terrace. Al and Jack suddenly spotted a table of six friends—other students from Oxford, they informed me—and suggested we join them. The food in Oxford was evidently even worse than it was in London, and the food at the university dining halls worse yet—so, if nothing else, these young men had come to Paris to eat. They could devour entire trays of cheese, drink carafes of young red wine, eat double portions of meat and end the meal by ordering any desert with the word "crème" in it. Recovering from their Sunday lunch, they were drinking coffee at the Mabillon. As we pulled up extra chairs, we exchanged introductions—Tom Blackburn and Brock Brower are the only two new names I remember now. Everyone started talking at once.

Barbara and Lin Stafford, back in Paris after several months in Japan, had already met Brock through a mutual friend and promised, repeatedly, to introduce me to him. But somehow, we had not met until that moment.

So this is Brock Brower, I said to myself. His sparkling blue eyes were looking at me and he had a smile on his face. I felt a rush of adrenaline, provoked simply by the appearance of this handsome young man. There was never any shortage of topics for conversation in Paris cafés. Well-seasoned travelers that we were, comparisons of life in Paris, London, Oxford and America could keep us occupied for hours. As we sipped our coffee, Brock turned to me and asked if I knew the Staffords. Yes, I did, and that began our talk, which seemed, as it went on, more and more our own private conversation. We were oblivious to the others at the table.

I looked at my watch and realized I was late for the phone call I'd promised myself I would make to my brother. Reluctantly excusing myself—thinking perhaps I should stay longer since I found the company so amusing—I rose from the table and, saying my goodbyes, shaking hands all around, started toward my hotel. As I got up, Brock stood too. He came up behind me, intent, it seemed, on walking with me. He said he was going to visit the Orangerie Museum. He didn't ask me to accompany him but in any event, I often went to the Orangerie and had more important things on my mind. So we said goodbye again and he rejoined his friends, all of whom were returning to Oxford the next day. Spring break was over, their vacation money spent.

I had a wistful sense of having missed something; I was sorry I would not see Brock again because he was so appealing—handsome and entertaining. The Staffords had given me all the details of his life—his excellent writing, his brilliant scholarship—and, oh yes, a sketch of his family and his wealthy, successful father, a famous advertising executive in New York. But events were pulling me in another direction—the phone call to Henry in Stuttgart, my determination to rethink my life, perhaps go back to graduate school in the States. With the arrival of spring, I was ready for a change. It was too late for him, no room in my life now. If only we'd met sooner. But then,

I mused, if it were meant to be… Besides, I wasn't sure he would like me if we actually sat down to talk. There was a touch of arrogance about him, evident even at our first meeting.

At the hotel I had to wage a particularly intense struggle to persuade Madame Gullies that my long distance phone call was urgent. She finally gave her permission, hovering around the phone during the entire conversation to make sure I placed only one call. During that call to Stuttgart, Henry explained to me that he needed $300 to pay his gambling losses, a tidy sum in 1955. I didn't hesitate to say I would send it immediately. That settled, I had the hotel maid fill the hotel's one bathtub with steaming hot water and let the last of my malaise disappear with a leisurely soak.

The next morning was again warm and sunny, a welcome change for a city where winter's darkness had ruled so long. I felt unusually bouyant as I headed for a taxi to take me to rue Scribe. American Express still has its office on rue Scribe, but it is nothing like the mecca it was in the 1950s. It was a lifeline for expatriates and students, connecting them to family and friends in the States. They picked up their mail at American Express if they were in transit—and when money was involved, it was their bank.

I walked through the revolving door onto the cool marble floors and up to the barred cashier's window, three hundred dollars in francs in my purse. The office was as formal as any bank and had a comforting atmosphere of security. You could trust American Express—it was an institution and Americans trusted their institutions then.

With help from an obliging clerk, I filled out my telegram to my brother and the money went winging to Stuttgart. Henry did not have to go to the brig, though his feckless Army career never took a turn for the better. He was given the job as the colonel's driver and, much to his superior's disgust, again and again would forget to fill the gas tank. On one particularly difficult day as he sat at the wheel waiting for the colonel, he idly popped open the glove compartment. There was a handgun inside which he pulled out. He examined it carefully and, assuming it had to be unloaded (a concealed weapon, after all), pulled the trigger. The bullet lodged in the dashboard, fortunately. The colonel never mentioned the incident after the first shock of discovery, but my brother was relieved of his job and spent the rest of his Army career typing in the adjutant's office. The Army had brought him to Europe, however, and I was overjoyed to have a member of my family on the continent.

When the Staffords later met my brother during his first visit to Paris, they enraged him by saying, "You could be a male model." He was a perfect template for tall, dark and handsome. His complexion tanned perfectly and he was funny and charming. But he took his masculinity seriously, and no one was going to call him a "pretty boy." He was insulted and couldn't leave their company fast enough.

I must admit that being able to bail out my brother was a power trip. When we were teenagers (he was three years younger than I), he always made money with his part-time jobs while I seemed unable to afford a pack of cigarettes. He has repaid me for my single act of generosity a thousandfold with countless loans—most, but not all, repaid.

As I was leaving American Express, Brock Brower was entering. "I thought you were going back to England," I said, smiling, very surprised to see him. "Well yes," he replied. "I'm waiting for some mail—a letter from my father. It was supposed to be here yesterday."

At that point, I turned to continue on my way out the door, and Brock stopped me. "Wait for me outside," he said. "We can have a cup of coffee after I get the mail." So I waited, standing on the sunlit sidewalk outside American Express, for the rest of my life to begin.

We found the perfect small café, shaded by a dark green awning that had just been unrolled, and the conversation we'd begun at the Mabillon the day before continued seamlessly. I expected him to announce that his departure was imminent and to watch as he rushed off to catch the train to London but instead he said, "I'll be here one more night. Why don't we have dinner?"

He arrived at the Hotel Welcome at about six o'clock and we walked slowly down Boulevard Saint-Germain, through the long shadows of the setting sun, joining the Parisian strollers who crowded the sidewalks. It was a moment when anyone would have felt that it was wonderful to be in Paris. My love affair with the city was a fait accompli. This new attraction in my life, Brock, was still being played out.

Our destination was Bemelman's, a quaint bistro on Île Saint-Louis, named for the writer and illustrator of the Madeleine stories for children. Crossing the Pont Neuf to the Île de la Cité, we continued along the quais that bordered the Seine, watching a *bateau mouche* glide slowly past, its tiny, sparkling white lights reflected in the water. The sky had taken on its evening glow—cerulean blue with faint streaks of pink clouds.

Bemelman's had no more than a dozen tables crowded into its small interior. The walls were decorated with murals painted by Bemelman himself, vignettes from his Madeleine books. Recessed lighting from the low ceilings lit the murals and the candles on each table cast long, flickering shadows among the files of little girls in their wonderful round brimmed hats. Our multicourse meal was accompanied by a bottle of Rosé de Provence. In time it would become our favorite wine, something we thought we'd discovered together—a gentle, pale, rose-colored touch of grape. The meal itself was delicious, but its effect was blurred by our talk and laughter. We seemed to agree about everything of any significance in our lives. We would never be encumbered by possessions, agreeing that travel was much more important to our happiness than houses and gardens. And things. Aside from books, we would never need to clutter our lives with belongings. As for money, it was not even worthy of a mention in our exalted version of the future. Our future? Already it seemed assumed that it would, somehow, be ours.

Holding hands, we left the restaurant and began the walk back to Saint-Germain. It took us, in this walker's city, through lle de la Cite and back across the Pont Neuf. The sky was completely dark now and the bridge was lit with large globes of white light on handsome embossed iron posts. The Seine, marbled with dots of reflected light, flowed placidly beneath us. The early spring air was still warm. Suddenly, Brock stopped and asked me to sit on the stone wall of the bridge. As I did so, he stood back, surveying me carefully. Is something wrong? I wondered.

Finished with his analysis, he moved toward me and with his index finger, carefully and gently removed the pale blue eye shadow I was wearing from each eyelid. "There," he said. "That's better." I was bemused by his gesture and in my newfound euphoria, perfectly content to interpret it as one of affection. If this were a hint of a controlling personality that might later emerge, it was far from my thoughts that night. I was flattered to think he cared for me and not my makeup—and more important, he seemed to be discarding my fashion image for one of substance, the real me. Back at the hotel, we passionately kissed good night, thoroughly engrossed in each other. Brock had again changed his plans and was staying on in Paris. We agreed to meet for lunch the following day.

And the next day and the next—lunch and dinner, long walks in the beautiful April weather. After five days, I was hopelessly in love—and very sad to think he would be leaving me to return to Oxford, where he was reading English. settled into his other life, about which I knew nothing.

On April 18, the day he finally left for England, I wrote my first letter to him:

My dear Brock,

As I turned the key to my room, I felt terribly lonely and almost as if I didn't want to go in. Then I saw the book and the flowers that you had left for me. I had felt, during the afternoon, much more desperate than I thought I would. And when I returned there was something to reassure me; something to prove that it wasn't nebulous or imaginary—that I did know you and love you.

I have always accepted leave takings as natural phenomena. My reasoning was something to the effect that one meets people and sometimes it matters. Still, you see them leave—or you leave yourself—and within a few hours nothing remains but a vague memory. Vague memories are easily forgotten. I found out today that it is not always so effortless. If my memory of any part of that week becomes vague, I resent it.

Now, I am very sleepy and irritated because this—words and paper—is somehow inadequate. Perhaps when I am more accustomed to knowing you, I will be able to write and feel like saying something besides, "I love you." But now, I haven't another thought in my head. Except that I wonder where you are and what you are doing. By this time, you are probably asleep and I myself will be soon.

How much I miss you!

All my love, Ann

# 10

## Romance in the Fifties

In his first letter to me, Brock included an invitation to join him for Eights Weekend, Oxford University's traditional May social event. The weekend takes its name from the sculls, each with eight rowers, that are entered by every university college in the spring race. A week of competitions is capped by the final race on a Saturday, a mad dash on the Isis River. I was eager to see Oxford and the town it had made famous. It was not lost on me that almost six centuries of academic history separated Oxford, England and Oxford, Ohio.

The weekend promised to be a celebration of both the new season and the proximity of summer vacation, a giddy student revel overflowing with champagne and sherry. It began when Brock met me at the Oxford train station. We left my suitcase at my hotel and walked to his ground floor suite at Merton College. I was unprepared for the cozy comfort of his rooms. The living room fireplace was kept stacked with fresh wood by his scout, a male caretaker provided by the college, and there was a separate bedroom and bath—impressive accommodations for a graduate student.

Merton College has staked its claim as the oldest college at Oxford. The beauty of its ivy-cloaked, gray stone medieval buildings, with its landmark Gothic chapel and tower, is undeniable. Free of the frequent misty rains typical of English spring and summer, it proved a perfect backdrop for romance.

For the Saturday race, each college had moored a barge at the river's edge with awnings and lawn chairs so spectators could watch in regal comfort, decorously sipping tall flutes of champagne, fresh strawberries floating in them. As the sculls appeared, their passage was attended by loud cheering, everyone urging on the favorite boat. It was a grand spectacle, embellished with the staccato sounds of our buoyant talk and laughter in the full sunshine.

One of the best attended events of the weekend was a production of Brock's verse play, *The Tender Edge*, performed in the medieval Merton College dining room. It was a bittersweet drama of young romantic love that made the dreamy quality of the balmy spring weekend even more poignant. Not only was Brock handsome and charming; he was also extremely talented.

Brock's tutor, Hugo Victor Dison-Dison, seemed like the quintessential Oxford don. A gnomish, balding man recently widowed, he was known for his inebriating sherry parties. Once he met me, his favorite game was to corner me and, looking up from his small stature, ask about my "Cinderella story"—meeting the American prince in a Paris café. He was a bit of a snob, but I found his waspish tongue amusing. When Brock told Hugo he'd been awarded a First by the examining committee, Hugo congratulated him with a resounding "Well done, you old devil." He was pleased and surprised that his American student had done so well. Years later, when Brock and I were watching *Darling*, a movie starring Julie Christie, we were astounded to see the college don played by Hugo himself. We agreed it was perfect casting.

During that spring weekend, Brock unveiled his plans for a six-week summer tour of Europe—his long vacation—and asked me to accompany him. I was unable to respond immediately—stunned by the invitation, coming as it did without any trappings: no engagement ring, no commitment. I was equally surprised that he had already made elaborate and detailed plans for the trip. He had carefully prepared the itinerary and we spent several hours poring over maps and guide books. He planned to begin in Nice in August, then follow the French and Italian Riviera, swing inland to Florence and Tuscany, Rome and Naples, then down the Amalfi Coast to Sorrento, Capri and Positano. The trip would continue by boat from Brindisi to Greece and the Greek Islands. By June Brock would have his own car, a gift from his father. He had decided to get a Morris Minor sedan, giving us all we needed for a luxury land cruise. It promised to be a picture-perfect idyll. I was definitely thrilled to be included, but cautious too. It could be wonderful or disastrous beyond imagination. Yet, in the end, I happily accepted.

With the champagne bottles emptied, the weekend came to an end. My vague plans to return to America and enter graduate school were easily traded for another year of continental life. I returned to Paris and a full calendar of modeling assignments. *Vogue* offered me a contract to model the all couturiers' *prêt-a-porter* collection for fall, a bit of good luck since the work would pay my share of the grand tour. My photographs filled a dozen pages in *Vogue*'s September Collection issue.

When he heard about our proposed trip, my father wrote to me saying, "It sounds like an unusual opportunity to see Europe, but if you have any hopes for the future of the relationship, I would advise against it." I considered his advice thoughtfully and then decided it was nonsense. My father's cautions expressed the normal parental desire that my serious romance would lead to marriage. I was too blissfully happy, however, to worry about the future. At that point in my life, traveling with Brock was easier without a commitment. I was in no mood to make any life-changing decisions.

I had watched my friends fall in love without fear of the consequences. It was not that easy for me. A dark negative lingered in my mind of bitter marital battles, of contentment eroded when meager income couldn't pay the bills. The effect of my mother's illness on her marriage and family was simply devastating, only adding complexity to the simplest of domestic rituals. In spite of that, my parents managed to share many happy years, but I was still dwelling on my own emotional scars. This was not to my credit, but it helped make me an easy target for a summer fling.

Both Brock and I were intrepid travelers. We would lunch in olive groves overlooking the Mediterranean with, literally, a loaf of bread and wine; dine at inexpensive and carefully chosen restaurants and sightsee while clutching our constant companion, the informative and meticulously detailed Fodor Guide. We were a matched pair, dreamers with freedom and mobility. Travel light and travel fast became our credo. Two such liberated souls would be hard to find again.

# Chapter 10

When the two weeks of photo shoots for *Vogue* ended in early August, I took the Train Bleu to Nice where Brock met me. Filling the back seat and trunk of the still shiny black Morris Minor with sleeping bags (which we used only once), suitcases and books, we began our drive along the Riviera. Southern France and Italy were blessed with hot summer weather. At one point we spent two days with Holly and Jack Massee who were tenting with their children on the then tranquil beach in Saint-Tropez. Brock met them for the first time and liked them as much as I did. We felt completely carefree and, as Brock's father wrote us, were living like "a couple of happy apes in a rose tree." (He liked to mix his genius for advertising slogans with his parental wit and wisdom.) Like my father, he found it hard to believe we were not thinking about the future.

From the coast of Italy we drove to Florence, stopping in Pisa just long enough to see the leaning tower since we didn't relish shouldering our way through dozens of other tourists. Our routine was simple. We would arrive at our destination by late afternoon, open the Fodor Guide, its pages filled with descriptions of tourist attractions, and see as much as possible before wandering the streets of whatever village or city we were in, searching for the perfect restaurant. By the time our late dinner was finished, we were more than ready to fall asleep in the inexpensive hotel we had booked on arrival. In the morning, we bought bread, salami or ham, provolone cheese and fresh fruit for a midday picnic and, if we were leaving that day, would pile into the Morris Minor and take off. To dilute the boredom of long drives (though the curves and heights of Italian roads didn't leave much room for ennui), I would read aloud from one of the books we'd brought while Brock drove.

We read Henry James' *Daisy Miller*, J.D. Salinger's *Nine Stories* and for nonfiction, another fifties' best seller, A.C. Spectorsky's *The Exurbanites*, proving to ourselves that we were Americans first and tourists second.

After five days in Florence, we still had not exhausted its art and architectural treasures. Finally, we tore ourselves away and headed south to Siena. It was a beautiful day, a full sun drying the puddles of the overnight thunderstorm. To our amazement, the cobbled streets of Siena were completely empty when we arrived. A hushed, expectant silence hung over the small city as we stopped near a carved stone fountain, centered in a square decorated with vivid flowers. We were about to descend down a narrow, heavily shadowed lane when, suddenly, a parade of horses and riders in medieval trappings, the riders waving large colorful flags, burst into the sunlit square. In a matter of seconds, the tiny square was filled with riders energetically whipping their horses to a gallop while shouting, singing crowds followed in their wake. With all exits blocked, it was impossible to move our car, so we abandoned it and followed the crowds to a large arena with a racetrack. We were suddenly part of a flood of people, spilling into the middle of the arena. It would have been impossible to go against the pressing tide of the crowd.

It was August sixteenth, the day of the famous Palio del Contrade, a horse race that dates back to the Eleventh Century. Before beginning the drive to Siena, we had failed, for the first time, to consult our guide and our calendar. This dramatic scene was our novel introduction to a world-class event. It was a glorious spectacle but also a frightening encounter with the powerful surge of masses of people.

By the time we got to Rome, the heat was oppressive and we were anxious to return to the seacoast. But Rome was exciting, its crowded streets clogged with traffic that white-uniformed policemen tried to control with whistles. At the Roman Baths we saw a performance of *Aida* that was like a grand opera circus—elephants, camels and divas all parading across the stage. Using a map in the Fodor, we wandered the Forum, trying to imagine its ancient grandeur. There was so much to see, so many charming cafés and restaurants, that we stayed longer in Rome than we had intended. Fortunately, we had a flexible schedule.

When we did leave, we drove south to Naples, then along the Amalfi Coast, visiting Sorrento, Positano, Amalfi and Ravello, a quartet of antique villages carved out of the rocky Mediterranean coast. A brief one-day boat trip gave us a glimpse of Capri. There was also time for a day trip to Pompeii. Since we had so carefully recreated the buildings of the Roman Forum, we had to apportion an equal amount of time to the remnants of life in ancient Pompeii. I was beginning to long, however slightly, for a taste of my glamorous Paris life. Luckily, our energy seemed inexhaustible despite the intense August heat.

Our only near accident occurred on the road to Brindisi when, hurtling along at top speed after dark, we almost crashed into a horse-drawn cart with only one dim light bobbing behind. By the time we arrived in Brindisi, a small seaport on the Adriatic coast, we were suffering from severe travel fatigue and finally booked a luxury hotel.

The ship scheduled to take us to Athens would not leave until late afternoon, so we wandered along the waterfront, looking for diversion. There was a cluster of small rowboats at the pier, every boat owner begging the few tourists to take a short trip around the harbor. We signaled to an old man and his young grandson that we would like a short trip in their rowboat. The Adriatic was placid and calm. The irresistible little boy, about eight years old, bounded out of the boat and held his hand out to help me climb in. *"Lui parla Inglesie,"* the man said, proudly pointing to the boy. He speaks English! bounded out of the boat and gave me his hand to help me climb in. I was instantly won over. His large brown eyes were so expressive and there was such a sweet, mutually supportive tie between the boy and the older man. The grandfather rowed while his grandson talked, and it was obvious that his command of English was greatly admired by the old man. The boy looked at us and asked me if we were "Marry-ed." as he pronounced it. "Oh, no." I laughed, genuinely amused by his precocious question. He looked solemnly at me, then at Brock, then back to me again. "Ees your father a goud father?" he finally asked, carefully enunciating each word. I was embarrassed to realize that I was not only breaking my own country's taboos—for that was easy—but also those of his country. And that required more explanation. My brief reply did not reflect the complexity of my thoughts. "Yes, my father is a good father." He was silent after that, as we rowed back to shore. But I'm sure he wondered how a good father could let his daughter travel with a young man to whom she was not married. It was much too difficult to explain that, in fact, my father did not want me to take the trip with Brock. I, for better or for worse, wasn't listening to anyone's advice, least of all mundane cautions from my good father. There was no way to dispel the boy's visions of licentious couplings with a description of our timid and only partially successful ventures into the sexual side of our relationship. Our romance was still tentative and it was hard to believe that our attempts at closeness could be considered against the rules.

After an exhausting overnight boat trip when we slept fitfully on deck chairs, we arrived in Piraeus, the port for Athens. It was September and Athens was smoggy and fiery hot by noon. It turned out to be inadvisable to leave the hotel room except in early morning and late afternoon. For partial protection, we bought hats to shield us from the boiling sun and headed out. In 1955 tourists were still allowed to trample the ancient stones of the Acropolis, giving them a chance to see the restored remains of building and statues at close range. A spreading panoramic view of the city was visible from the crest of the hill. We were in awe of the sight, the precision of the carvings and statues of ancient Greeks that managed to be both monumental and realistic. Athens itself felt more foreign than any other city we had visited. Even with its overlay of Western culture, the Middle Eastern influences burned through, insisting on their share of the Mediterranean sun.

Our side trip to Delphi exposed us to the chaos of Greek bus travel, a hot, dusty and overcrowded mode of transportation. By pure chance, we arrived the night that Rice Stephens, the famous Metropolitan Opera coloratura, was performing *Orpheus and Eurydice*, the Richard Strauss opera, at the outdoor amphitheater. Listening to the arias under a starry summer sky made us forget the occasional hardships of travel.

On our return to Athens, we went immediately to the port of Piraeus to board another shabby Greek ship for a tour of the Cyclades Islands. The captain was a tall, snarling man with a cigar hanging out of his mouth. He shouted orders and was equally rude to both passengers and crew. Unluckily, about forty members of the Club Mediterranee were embarking for the islands on the same ship. They arrived earlier than we did and had not only commandeered all the deck chairs but eaten all the food available for lunch and eventually for dinner as well. There were only three staterooms on the ship, all occupied, so we unrolled our sleeping bags and slept on the deck.

After dark, a few of the Greek sailors insisted on teaching us a raucous hornpipe dance before we crawled into our sleeping bags. The personnel on the boat were jolly and welcoming, but the accommodations were miserable. A strong wind had whipped the sea into a froth and the small ship was barely able to steady itself. By the time we arrived at the Mykonos harbor, Brock was much too seasick for further travel. We never reached our ultimate destination, Santorini, the volcanic isle where donkeys took visitors to the village on the hill. We could barely manage to stagger off the boat at Mykonos and collapse in a small hotel on the wharf.

The Mediterranean sun spread like melted crystal over the dome-shaped, whitewashed stucco houses, lending the island an ethereal glow. Like mushrooms sprouting on the rocks, its houses grew up the hillside, flanking steep stairways leading to cliffs above the sea. From their homes, weavers sold bolts of brilliantly colored wool and cotton, their hand looms visible through open doorways.

Once the wind died and the sea was calm, islanders rowed us to Delos, the tiny satellite island where the only inhabitants were remnants of ancient Greek sculpture and crumbling altars to their gods. On another day, we packed a picnic lunch and rowed to a solitary rock outcropping not far from shore, where we swam and lay in the scalding sun. Mykonos was still tranquil in the fifties, largely undiscovered by tourists. It was the perfect island retreat, a place I loved almost more than my traveling companion.

The return trip from mainland Greece to Italy was rigorous. This time I was the one who was sick, and Brock forced the captain to give me an officer's bunk where I could sleep off the most acute phase of my illness, which was diagnosed as mild dysentery once we got to dry land. Our cheap hotel in Athens was simply not clean and unfortunately we shared a bathroom with other guests in the hotel. But a very fatherly doctor in Brindisi gave me the necessary antibiotic and within two days, I had fully recovered.

Brock picked up the Morris Minor that he had left in Brindisi and we drove along the west coast of Italy to Venice. We had been traveling for five weeks. Happy tourists, we drifted in gilded gondolas through canals shaded by walls of Renaissance architecture and joined the pigeons in the Piazza San Marco, marveling at its colors and texture. The rest of our trip went quickly. By October, I found myself back in Paris, faced with the necessity of reviving my modeling career and, this time, watching Brock leave for his second year at Oxford.

Once I had become attached to him, I began to hate being alone. It was as if my courage had suddenly disappeared. I longed to be with him, and this became a burden to both of us. I was infatuated with his ambition, his talents and his mastery. Even Paris seemed dull and tasteless after such a whirlwind summer. I had no choice but to air out my hotel room, call

Madame Dillet at *Vogue* and begin modeling again even though my glamourous career was becoming shopworn.

Had timing dictated a different sequence of events, had a serious, committed relationship with another man come earlier, I might never have gone to Paris in the first place. My adventure, my invention of a new life in a foreign country, was predicated on being alone. From the moment I set sail, everything I did involved risk. My yearning for the security of a committed relationship was just beginning to surface. When it hit, it swept me away. Once I had fallen in love, no rational argument could make me change my mind. Were we right for each other? Were his withdrawals into sad silence a warning or a comfort? Was his close relationship with his parents, brother and sister a sign of well established independence or inability to separate? I felt I'd lived at least nine lives since I had left home in September. I was an independent young woman who had proved my ability to survive in the real world and I knew my own mind—and my own strength. At least, that's what I thought.

In actuality, I was probably less prepared for the cloister of marriage than most twenty-something women. I wanted to give up my modeling career, not altogether a wise decision, to become a journalist. Beyond that, I was tormented by uncertainty. I had separated from my family, but only geographically. The more fraught the emotional tangles, the harder the break. And I had barely begun the psychic labor of that task. At the very least, I was totally unprepared to do anything that would remotely resemble "settling down."

By November, my misgivings forgotten, Brock and I became formally engaged. For an entire weekend in Paris, we searched carefully for a ring. At Cartier on the place Vendome, a gentle clerk opened a velvet case filled with brilliant stones. We chose a perfect small sapphire and two smaller diamonds that would have made a beautiful ring. But Brock was still a student and the stones were more than he could afford. We ended our search when I decided against the single pearl ring he could afford. Having both accepted our commitment to the other, we decided there was no need for an engagement ring after all.

# 11

# Le Quatorze Juillet

The Fourteenth of July is capitalized only in France, where it assumes great historical importance as the day in 1789 when the antiroyalists stormed the Bastille, an archaic prison filled with political dissenters and not a few out and out criminals. In France today, the event is celebrated as the beginning of the Free Republic, with grand displays of fireworks watched by thousands from the bridges of the Seine. Dancing in the streets, boisterous revelers keep the city alive until dawn.

The day Brock and I chose to get married in Oxford, England, just happened to be July fourteenth, 1956, an ordinary Wednesday in Great Britain, Bastille Day in France. It was the hiatus between Brock's final "viva," as his appearance before the examining committee of the college was called, and the Oxford University graduation ceremony.

Three months before the wedding, I rented an apartment in South Kensington and made a permanent move to London. I would miss Paris and French cuisine, but I would never miss the rustic accommodations of the Hotel Welcome. I had Jean Smith, an excellent London modeling agent, who worked tirelessly to keep me booked almost every day. By that time, there were far more modeling jobs for me on the English side of the Channel.

I arranged our modest wedding ceremony in what was becoming my trademark style—alone. I wrote the invitations by hand on ivory vellum. I found my white lace, empire waist, cocktail length dress after much searching in a boutique on Old Bond Street in Mayfair. It was carefully fitted to my thin body by one of the Queen's seamstresses. I made my own cap, a lacy white headband interwoven with satin ribbon. This bride would not be shrouded in any veils. I asked Holly Massee to be my matron of honor and she instantly accepted. Brock chose his friend Robert Paxton, another Rhodes Scholar and fellow Mertonian, to be his best man. Boyish-looking and quite southern (his family owned a newspaper in Lexington, Virginia), Bob was a French history student, precociously on his way to becoming a brilliant scholar and writer.

Brock's parents were already in Oxford to attend his graduation as well as our wedding. My father was in Italy, lecturing on art and archaeological history to a student tour from Miami University. He arrived two days before the ceremony in a highly anxious state. He was terribly afraid of flying and the trip had been unusually stormy and bumpy. The fact that my mother was not attending the wedding also worried him. I knew from painful experience that she would have been dangerously stressed had she tried to come. I was adamant that I be spared her inevitably manic presence at the ceremony. Even with my unyielding decision to be married without her, I could not avoid the sadness this decision caused. I was determined not to be sentimental, but I felt we had somehow abandoned each other. Neither of us wanted to feel ashamed.

Fortunately, my Uncle Kenneth arrived from New York and rented the Mercedes that took me to the church. He and my father joined forces to purchase a dozen place settings of sterling silver flatware, in a pattern of our choice, for a wedding present. His polished New York charm and his financial success made him a perfect companion for my professorial father, his younger brother. He added a light touch of confidence to an event that was freighted with some heavy overtones.

There were several reasons for our decision to be married in England, my mother's ongoing psychological problems being only one of them. The fact that all our mutual friends were still in either England or France was important to us. I happily adopted Oxford, England and a small medieval church called St. Peter-in-the-East as the site for the wedding. With its Gothic nave and square Norman tower, it was architecturally unique. In the 1970s, St. Peter's was renovated, retaining its stone-carved gargoyles, to serve as a library for St. Edmund Hall, one of the Oxford University colleges.

I saw myself as a calm, purposeful bride, less interested in ritual than result. The sooner all ceremony ended, the happier I would be. Yet I fussed so much over the size of my white bouquet that Holly got angry and, pushing the clump of flowers in my hand, said, "Take it and get going down the aisle!" My idea of a "simple, small" wedding couldn't extend to everything.

The weather on our wedding day was typical of England in midsummer, with overcast skies and mist in the air. The English believe it is good luck to be married in the rain, more a reflection of the island's summer climate than a matter of faith. As the ceremony began at noon and I walked down the aisle on my father's arm, the sun appeared. Our fifty guests, half filling the church, stood to watch our progress to the altar. The chaplain from Maudlin College, an intense young man, officiated at our ceremony. It followed the traditional pattern except that I had elected to change the phraseology of "to love, honor and obey." My solemn vow was "to love and honor each other."

There was enough to make any bride nervous. My new in-laws were kind but hardly in a relaxed frame of mind. They had graciously accepted me as a new member of the family, but they were somewhat mystified by my modeling career. They would have preferred a graduate of one of the Seven Sisters colleges. At moments, the aura of their carefully concealed disapproval shadowed the event. The groom was busy thinking about himself and his own response to ritual, in this case the proper toast to the bride at the reception. At one point in the ceremony when we were supposed to kneel before the attar, he slumped down, resting back on his heels. I found myself towering above him in a proper posture, forced to duplicate what he was doing so I wouldn't feel ridiculous. We stood to exchange our vows and Brock slipped a wide, carved gold ring on my finger. (We had found the Victorian ring in a London antique store and when I tried it on in the shop, it fit me perfectly.) Inside, it was engraved with our names and the date of our wedding.

Our guests waited patiently in their seats while we signed the registry in a small room beside the altar, laughing and talking with Brock's parents and my father. Everyone sighed with relief as we finally walked back down the aisle, man and wife.

# Chapter 11

The Studley Priory, the large stone country inn we had chosen for the reception, perched high on a hill overlooking the bucolic English countryside. It had actually once been a nunnery, before Henry the Eighth burned it to the ground during one of his anti-Catholic purges. But that was centuries ago. In this century, the stone mansion, rebuilt by an English squire, was transformed into a small castle-like hotel. Brock's toast to me was a witty and thoughtful reminder of our romantic "tale of two cities," London and Paris. Keeping to the established rituals, we jointly cut through the white icing of the wedding cake, surprised to discover a brown spice cake inside. The cake, true to English tradition (not ours), was something of a shock, as I had intended it to be white. There were more toasts, one from Brock's father, one from my urbane Uncle Kenneth, and a simple "To Brock and Ann" from my father. During the reception there was an awkward moment when a butler came up to me asking if I wanted to order more champagne. It had disappeared at a much more rapid rate than I had anticipated. I said yes. After all, I was paying all the bills.

Months before our wedding, Norman Parkinson's advice to both Brock and me cautioned us to accept each other as we were. "It's useless to try to change another person," he said insistently. His sage advice would come back to haunt us. We were a crafty pair, secretly determined to mold the other to the shifting contours and behavior of our ideal mate. I was never one to follow good advice.

\* \* \* \*

The past is overshadowed by the present. Retrieving it is like peering through the wrong end of a telescope, focusing on tiny objects in a constricted frame, enlarging them with memory and imagination. I originally wrote this memoir to put capricious memory into a more enduring form. As I wrote, another reason appeared—to learn something about my short voyage on the planet and the self that had committed to that voyage. But perhaps the most joyous reason for writing a memoir is to break away briefly from the confines of the present into the world of the past.

One friend said, "But how do you remember? I've forgotten everything." I assured her that she hadn't forgotten, just misplaced. The human brain is always recording and storing information. For years, I assumed that life was a slow process of loss. In fact, it is a rapid process of gain. One has only to connect the dreams and memories and miraculously, the past can be lived again.

# About the Author

Ann Montgomery began writing *Another Me* when she was a Georgetown realtor in Washington, DC. She worked on the manuscript for twelve years. This is her first book. She has written for *More* magazine and *The Princeton* (New Jersey) *Packet* and is a published poet. A native of Oxford, Ohio, she graduated from Miami University and lives in Santa Barbara, California and Norwich, Vermont. Visit the author's website: www.AnotherMeMemoir.com

www.AnotherMeMemoir.com

Printed in the United States
137191LV00003B/18/P